Climate Change and the Creative Economy in India

Weaving has been a significant aspect of India's cultural and economic history. Climate change is increasingly affecting crucial relationships within the weaver communities. This book explores the dialectical relationship between the craft of weaving and the changing climate.

Exploring questions of how climate variabilities are affecting local geographies and weaving ecosystems, the book discusses case studies of creative economy clusters in India. The author employs ethnographic fieldwork to share lived and embodied experiences of climate change.

This concise book will be useful reading to scholars, researchers and students with an interest in the creative and cultural industries and how these intersect with environmental issues and climate change.

Pragya Sharma is a Doctoral Researcher in History of Design at the University of Brighton, UK.

Routledge Focus on the Global Creative Economy
Series Editor: Aleksandar Brkić,
Goldsmiths, University of London, UK

This innovative Shortform book series aims to provoke and inspire new ways of thinking, new interpretations, emerging research, and insights from different fields. In rethinking the relationship of creative economies and societies beyond the traditional frameworks, the series is intentionally inclusive. Featuring diverse voices from around the world, books in the series bridge scholarship and practice across arts and cultural management, the creative industries and the global creative economy.

Youth Culture and the Music Industry in Contemporary Cambodia
Questioning Tradition
Darathtey Din

Global Crisis and the Creative Industries
Analysing the Impact of the Covid-19 Pandemic
Ryan Daniel

Creative Economy and Sustainable Development
The Context of Indian Handicrafts
Madhura Dutta

Music Artist Managers
Remuneration and Retention in the Popular Music Business
Guy Morrow

Climate Change and the Creative Economy in India
Disadvantaged, Disturbed and Dislocated Indian Weavers
Pragya Sharma

For more information about this series, please visit: www.routledge.com/Routledge-Focus-on-the-Global-Creative-Economy/book-series/RFGCE

Climate Change and the Creative Economy in India

Disadvantaged, Disturbed and Dislocated Indian Weavers

Pragya Sharma

Routledge
Taylor & Francis Group
LONDON AND NEW YORK

First published 2025
by Routledge
4 Park Square, Milton Park, Abingdon, Oxon OX14 4RN

and by Routledge
605 Third Avenue, New York, NY 10158

Routledge is an imprint of the Taylor & Francis Group, an informa business

British Library Cataloguing-in-Publication Data
A catalogue record for this book is available from the British Library

ISBN: 978-1-032-58432-4 (hbk)
ISBN: 978-1-032-58438-6 (pbk)
ISBN: 978-1-003-45006-1 (ebk)

DOI: 10.4324/9781003450061

Typeset in Times New Roman
by SPi Technologies India Pvt Ltd (Straive)

Contents

Acknowledgements

As my first book, I hold a lot of gratitude for all the people who made this study a possibility. Conducting fieldwork in remote areas may not always be an easy undertaking. My friend and confidante Rishika Singh has always been the perfect co-traveller in heat and sweat, in the hubbub of train stations and in gulping down endless cups of tea – thank you for being ever ready to accompany me on trips even at a week's notice and to never saying no to whatever the research demanded, including walking on the railway tracks only because I wanted to witness a finishing process I spotted from a moving train. Rishika was also my Bangla translator.

I am indebted to the artisans for their generosity and support before, during and after the interviews. In Bengal – Biren Kumar Basak, Phooli Biswas, Rekha Biswas, Hazari Sheikh, Deepak and Archana Rajvanshi. In Kutch – Umaid Shree Bhai, Hamirji Vishram, Shamji Vishram, Premji Velji Siju, Naranbhai Siju, Namori Kaka, Siddharth Mangariya, Gopal Vankar, Vankar Poonam Arjan, Ranaji, Bhamal Jaimalji and Bhimji Velji Kanji. In Kerala – Manoharan, Prabhu, Anandan, Vasudevsan Ramalingam, Pradeep and Choundappan. I hope I have not missed anyone. I thank them for giving me their time in between their working hours at times in the middle of their afternoon siesta and for being so welcoming as I found myself at their workplaces. Their unassuming kindness is what kept me motivated when the weather or my temperament did not get on well with each other.

Thanks are also due to all the people who helped me connect with the weavers and share their own knowledge and lived experiences. At Phulia, Pranav Das, Niloy Das and Samir Das. In Kutch, Dhanji and Geeta prepared us warm meals and took care of our erratic food supplies. In Kuthampally, Subramaniam, who hosted us in his spare weaving room we stayed in and Gadha Gopal for translating my 'list' of questions, repetitively with the same fervour in every other interview.

Although the research and writing were undertaken in the last two years, this book has been in the making for much longer. As I pulled out old books and went through previous notes pasted along the edges of texts I have loved and revered, an unbroken thread ran through these – of nature, textiles, culture, communities, Indian history, and philosophy coursed through them is reflected in many parts of this book. I would not lie when I say that I often caught myself at a loose end. I wrote most of this manuscript while living in Brighton, braving my first English winter as I could be found typing away at my desk with thick chilblained fingers. In the UK's inclement weather, the experience of the changing climate was ever-present and felt.

Thanks are due to the Routledge team who happily consented for this book to have a language of its own and allow my 'personal' voice to be included in an academic context. Even thinking of conceiving and eventually writing and finishing this project would not have been possible were it not for Prof Saumya Pande who was also the first reader of this text. There are people who hand out your first ropes of research and she is that to me; thank you for being everything – a mentor, a guide, a friend, all at once. And lastly, I am short of words to express my gratitude towards my parents for never questioning my choices or my unwavering mind. This book is dedicated to them.

Glossary

abhivyakti	expression
ardaas	prayer
bhajan	devotional song or hymn
bunkar	a weaver in Western India
chador	a cloth covering for the body
charkha	spinning wheel
chutti	an interlocked detailing on the *pallu* that becomes an identifier of a Kuthampully handloom
desi	Indian, South Asian more broadly
desi oon	native wool including sheep wool or goat hair
dhabla	a draped garment that Rabari women wear
dhaaga	thread
fatka	shuttle
gamchha	a utilitarian multipurpose strip of cloth, forming an essential item in a tropical country
haat	a temporary local market
haath	hand, but used in the book, in context of a unit of length
jutis	a gender-neutral closed-toe handmade footwear, traditionally crafted from animal leather and often hand embroidered
kala cotton	a rain-fed cotton crop
kanji	a starch paste made from atta (whole wheat flour or bajra flour)
kapas	cotton
karai	color (in Malyalam)
kasavu	zari-like gold or silver thread; also the name of the Kerala sari
khilli	pegs, used in the context of warping done by women in Kutch
khoi	a starch paste made from boiled rice, sago starch and neem oil
kudrat	nature or ecology

ludi	an unstitched piece of textile that Rabari women wear; covers their heads and their backs
maad	starch
mahajan	traditionally a moneylender and in the present day an important linkage between the weaver and the end market
mandi	open market that sells fresh or local produce
mandili/mandali	a semi-formal group of singers performing in public
mann	soul
mausam	used interchangeably for weather and climate
nami	moisture
odhani/odhna	women's drape covering the back and the head
pallu/pallav	tail end of the sari that is taken over the shoulders and is left hanging at the back
parampara	tradition (also see *sanskruti*)
pashupaalak	animal keepers or herders
pavu	rolled cotton warp as is procured from Tamil Nadu
phooti kapas	a cotton variety that used to grow along the river basin and produced one of the finest textiles ever crafted by human fingers, known as muslin
sanskruti	tradition
sant	saint
sari	five and a half metres of undraped textile typified as the traditional attire for Indian women
soota	cotton thread
taar	individual threads in the warp
tant	frame or pit loom as referred to in Bengal
taana	the entire warp set
tanti	a weaver in the Bengal region
vrat	a crop that resembles an onion which was earlier used to starch desi oon

1 Introduction

Weaving as a skill is deemed older than the existence of the loom itself.[1] The craft can be considered autochthonous to India; the earliest weaving utilising cultivated cotton can be traditionally associated with India.[2] Constituting one of the largest cottage industries, the country is home to over two million handlooms.[3] Weavers are not merely artisans, manually operating the loom, pressing the treadle and throwing the shuttle, but in the interlacing of the warp and the weft, they find an expression of their immanent creativity. As makers, businesspersons and managers of their looms, weavers form an integral part of India's creative economy. And not just weavers, the handloom industry also engages spinners, warpers, warp sizers, bobbin winders, dyers, piece workers, tool makers and other ancillary workers. Weaving is the penultimate stage, before the textile is ready to be draped, but prior to it is an entire range of processes that the fibre goes through before it is ready to be woven, processes that are generally slotted into pre-loom and post-loom processes as enlisted above. As a country that exports textiles on a large scale, this army of skilled workers collectively produces 95% of the world's handwoven textiles.[4]

The Indian handloom sector is often described in common parlance as one that used to be a thriving industry and also one constantly viewed in a state of decline with reasons ranging from competition from power looms, fewer younger weavers choosing the loom as their workplace, escalating prices of raw materials and the atrocities of middlemen. This has led to weaning off, and in some cases obliteration, of traditional methods and processes, not just because new ways of knowing and doing (including technological innovations) have replaced the erstwhile tools and systems but also owing to the invisible and visible impacts of climate change that this introductory chapter will build the discussion on.

Handloom weaving stands only second to agriculture in supporting rural livelihoods in India. Localised making and selling have been the linchpin of this industry and thus inextricably linked with the village economy.[5] In the present context, the industry has been reorganised with

DOI: 10.4324/9781003450061-1

weavers working as part of cooperatives, societies or Self-Help Groups (SHGs) or as master weavers, independent weavers or job workers working for the master weavers.[6]

In South Asia, one of the easiest ways to initiate a conversation with a stranger is a discussion about *Mausam*, a word used interchangeably for weather and climate in India. It has been well recorded how one perceives a change in weather more intensely in areas where there is more dependence on ecological systems. "*Mausam mei kaafi badlaav aya hai*" (A lot of change in climate has happened) is a common refrain in India shared by many and a similar sentiment surfaced in most of my interviews as well.

Weaving follows the cyclical rhythms of seasons and the year as well as the rhythms of every day. For instance, in Bengal, humidity was conducive to the weaving of fine cotton muslin with weavers rising at dawn to work in the cool and increased humidity that early morning air offered.[7] Conversely, the dry hot climate of Tamil Nadu is suitable for weaving silks that require regulated temperature and humidity levels inside the weaving unit, with extremes of climate (hot, dry, damp and cold weather) causing easy breakage or sagging of the yarn.[8]

Spinning too has been sensitive to the climate of a region. It was earlier performed either in the morning or late afternoon when humidity was at its peak to keep the thread moist along with the precise tension and moisture imparted by the fingers – this was a necessary criterion. To intensify the humidity, spinners would also place water bowls around them to moisten the air or spin beside the inundated areas.[9] The surrounding water bodies thus played an important role in providing this extra humidity. In the off-monsoon season, with relatively less humidity, the thread became easily susceptible to damage. The monsoon brought a certain wetness to the atmosphere which was one of the reasons for the unique muslin produced in Bengal and this is evident in the naming of different varieties of muslin such as Abrawan, Nyansookh, Shabnum, Khassa and many others, based on levels of wetness.

For decades, weaving communities in India have faced the brunt of change propelled by the Industrial Revolution as well as natural calamities like droughts and famines that the subcontinent has always been prone to. They have also been vulnerable to the changing climate that creates fluctuations by interfering with the rhythms and patterns the weavers have always followed. Further, the practice of weaving cannot be left divorced from the practice of agriculture, the two acting as co-dependent activities. In pre-colonial South India, pre-loom tasks such as preparation of cotton or spinning of yarn were done by agriculturalists.[10] Instances in history abound of how the cotton famine of the early 1860s forced weavers to give up their looms or how the low agricultural productivity as a result of frequent droughts and famines in the late eighteenth and nineteenth century left the weavers wearied in spite of which they continued to persist, having learnt to subsist on scarcity.[11]

Events such as the climate crisis of the mid-1860s in Dharwad in Karnataka were not sudden or unexpected but largely occasioned by major forest clearance in Southern Konkan (that provided moisture) which caused the climate to become drier and seasons more uncertain.[12] Non-seasonal rainfall affects weaving practices by putting pauses in the active weaving season. Abrupt land winds affect the practice of weaving too with severe winds causing breakage of the warp yarns.[13] Additionally, many weaving communities used to utilise traditional methods to spin the yarn. For example, in Phulia, young girls would go into the fields before the sun rose when the dew drops were still intact and spin the yarn![14] These sets of knowledges are slowly disappearing from Indian weaving clusters.

The erratic climate patterns over the decades have coerced cotton farmers to revisit their choices with indigenous wisdom compelling them to return to old homegrown varieties of textile fibres, to revivify local cotton seeds and animal breeds. For instance, the increased use of kala cotton and desi oon in Kutch, which are more adaptable and resilient to climatic variabilities.[15] Earlier, most production cycles from fibre to textile were local, with the farmer growing cotton that was best suited to the local microclimate and local soil.[16] The different soils of the subcontinent were capable of germinating a multiplicity of cotton varieties, resulting in a hundred different kinds of Indian cloth.[17] Changes in technology in the handloom sector form another factor altering the climate – the automation of many processes and the shift from handloom to power loom and now Rapier looms make electricity an important part of their livelihood. Anthropocentric forces of such kind are slowly redefining the village environments.

Evidence exists among weaving clusters in India on how the changing climate is creating a sizeable impact on the handloom sector. The book explores this dialectical relationship between the craft of weaving and the changing climate, focusing on the everyday practice of weaving and other supporting activities. It will explore questions of how climate variabilities are affecting local geographies and weaving ecosystems via three case studies across weaving villages in East, West and South India.

Why Climate Change Matters to Craftspeople?

The craft of weaving involves manual bodily labour and is largely practised by rural craftspeople situated in disadvantaged and marginalised settings. Craftspeople have worked with the material affordances of what was available in their vicinity, relying on available natural resources, many of which are derived from forests. With the forest cover slowly reducing and tighter restrictions on access to this resource, there has been a gradual shift in traditional methods of working and the use of raw materials. The presence of a water body near their workplaces has been an intrinsic part of a weavers' settlement with the river water utilised in many pre-loom and post-loom processes.

A small change in climate can disrupt this fragile ecosystem with irreversible consequences along with a lot of time and resources spent on mitigation. As the effects are both visible and invisible, the experiences of the changing climate are both verbal and non-verbal. Weavers have always worked in accordance with changing weather patterns and are attuned to the changes in their environment in nuanced ways. As indirect chroniclers of the changing climate, weavers' perception of the environment becomes crucial to record because they have built a good understanding since most of them have resided in the same region all their lives.

India's weaving community holds precious, intangible, intergenerational knowledge that is largely practised as a hereditary occupation. Owing to the relationships weavers share with their environment, they are considered rich repositories of traditional knowledge. To intentionally steer away from the multiplicity of such terms and the associated conflicts, I have employed the term 'traditional knowledge' to refer to the valuable knowledge that is retained in oral traditions.[18] Especially because of the oral nature of this knowledge, it is often communicated using alternative metaphors and analogies. While explaining complex ideas or framing certain understandings of nature, weavers' frequent use of such allegories is a method in itself. The inhabitants of the three regions I interviewed had a profound understanding of the world around them, one could discover nuggets of wisdom hard to find across any written sources. This traditional (at times ancestral) wisdom, their ethos and the age-old knowledge of materials and processes constitute an important part of this research.

Historian Vijaya Ramaswamy calls this the weaver's 'native memory' regarding traditional techniques of making textiles that are as important to preserve if we are to sustain the handlooms.[19] Moreover, as I observed in my field research, local knowledge at the grassroots holds value only in that locale and can be activated only in that particular context. Once removed, they cease to hold any value which reasserts the importance of such knowledge. For this reason, I have retained the local colloquial terms for many of the techniques and processes that form the everyday vocabulary of the weavers. Where the English translation fails to do justice, especially in terms of the weaver's labour and skill, I have retained the word in the original language or dialect. In a similar vein have been retained honorifics such as *kaka* or *bhai* for a brother or inflexions such as *ji* that are appended to a person's name in many regions across India.

Apart from traditional knowledge, the book also focuses on autodidactic forms of knowledge. As a pan-country phenomenon and in its everydayness, weaving might appear as a deceptively simple operation but it requires coherent hand–body–mind coordination. The sophistication of handloom and the skill of the dextrous weaver collaborate to create the textile. Weaving (and spinning) is considered one of humanity's oldest forms of haptic engagement. The body of the weaver operates in tandem with the rhythms of the climate. This haptic knowledge embodied by the weavers cannot be communicated orally or in writing. A case in point is when I attempted to embody the weaver by sitting on a weaver's loom in the Gaurang Palli village in Phulia in Bengal and asked Mamoni Das, the woman weaver to teach me to weave. I was throwing the weft either too fast or too slow. The entire village soon teemed over, debating how exactly I should be passing the shuttle. I ended up breaking the thread a couple of times and Mamoni smilingly and deftly fixed it every time.

Weaving and Reciprocity

Beyond their environment, weavers share invaluable relationships with people as well that are essentially reciprocal in nature. Weaving as an everyday activity is a family-run enterprise; the working space becomes an extension of the home and vice versa. Not just the family, but members of the community including neighbours and relatives come in and assist in various steps and processes. Operating on multiple levels, the relationships with other communities have a considerable bearing on their weaving practice, imbuing it with meaning. For instance in Kutch, the Vankars (the weavers) of Bhujodi used to weave for the Rabaris (the pastoralists), who would exchange the textiles for grains or other food items in accordance with the weavers' needs of the time. And so, a repeated question I regularly found myself asking my interviewees was 'Who were the original wearers?' The book discusses how these relationships have either ceased to exist or no longer hold the same relevance.

Weavers also share reciprocal relationships with materials and processes – the materials are worked with and not worked upon.[20] The various stages of the weaving process not only require community involvement and ample raw materials procured from nature but also an ample amount of space to carry out the various activities. While weaving takes place inside, under a covered surface, pre-loom and post-loom activities such as sizing, warping, dyeing or washing often take place outdoors, in the open air.[21] Many of these processes can only be carried out during certain parts of the day and so fluctuations in weather can have a significant impact.

Another aspect that did not escape me throughout was how in all the three regions that this research is based on, the traditional and modern weaving spaces emanate from the ground. The ground thus becomes very important to the weavers as their surface of beginnings. This was also how I felt regarding other activities that were performed on a ground level – from sleeping on the floor to the stressed importance of eating by hand. I soon learnt that one understands a place more closely when it is traversed on foot and walked on and along. These mappings on foot considerably shaped many of the findings and where I could not walk the stretch, I opted for local means of transport such as rickshaws or trains.

The ideas and modes of worship of these weaving communities were something that could not be ignored either—how the bottom of a tree, a slab of stone or a corner of the road metamorphosed into a temple, with few sprinkling of flowers—these signs of obeisance are important to the research because, in a way by entering their villages and homes, I was entering their culture as well that reminded me of Geertz's definition of culture as a 'mode of thought'.[22] Instances such as these find space throughout this book, signalling the interconnectedness of work, worship and rituals.

The Practice of Weaving

Curator and historian Glenn Adamson writes in *The Invention of Craft* how craft is intrinsic to our being as a human.[23] Through the act of weaving, the weaver is not just surrendering his mind, fingers and entire body to the loom but the process speaks to the maker on a spiritual level as well. As Dipaka Maheta mentions in *Work, Ritual, Biography*, "in the production of cloth the cosmological ideas informing the world of weavers are expressed."[24] Eric Broudy writes about how the warp represents eternal existence while the weft is symbolic of the different stages of an individual's life.[25] The religious text Rigveda describes day and night as two female weavers 'intertwining the extended thread'.[26] The loom (and parts of it) finds itself as part of various folk songs of weaving communities across India. And so does the charkha (a traditional spinning wheel) which is often representative of the human body. In his poems, the subcontinent's mystic poet Kabir symbolised charkha as the wheel of life. Chapter 6 discusses in detail these musical engagements of the weaver with his loom in the Kutch region of Gujarat. Weaving then becomes not just material production but a form of cultural production as well.

Weaving as a practice is ritualised in India; it is hard to disassociate it from the various rituals and cultural practices of the region. Festivals and ceremonies in India always had relationships with the seasonal cycle. Weaving and agriculture are inextricably connected to the community's ritual calendars and so a changing climate is influencing these festivals and ceremonies too. For instance, in South India, during heavy monsoons, it becomes important to halt weaving for this period lest their looms and workspaces get inundated. This allowed festivals to be centred around this time. Will a changing climate in the coming years affect the timing of these festivals and ritual calendars?

Methodology

The research essentially relies on primary sources, through undertaking multi-sited fieldwork across the three weaving clusters. Semi-structured interviews, conversations that flowed into interviews and confabs became means to collect narratives of weavers, allied workers and other inhabitants of a region. I collected oral testimonies of not just people in an area but those residing in the neighbouring areas and their weaving spaces too – the inside and the outside. Other methods such as participant observation were employed, particularly in places where language posed a significant barrier as was the case in Nadia and Kuthampully. Particularly in the latter, where I had no familiarity with the language, it made me feel a bit disoriented, especially in long interviews.[27] Fortunately, I had friends who generously acted as mediators and translators. I soon realised that my limitations with the language at times aided in enhancing other sensorial skills, making me rely on acute observations, sound, perception, smell and touch.

Utilising the snowballing sampling method, the selection of interviewees was undertaken in the field. I was always conscious of moving beyond the gatekeepers who are more visible in the existing scholarship and instead including people whose voices have not been heard yet. This judgement while being in the field was crucial based on the time and financial constraints of this project.[28] Conducted in multiple languages – Hindi, English, Bengali, Kutchi, Malayalam and other dialects, the narrative accounts were transcribed and translated and later triangulated with both contemporary texts and historical sources. While writing this book, the personal became contextual since it is hard to detach or disassociate from the field I was charting. This makes the book accessible and readable by a wider demographic. I have avoided being the language too jargony making this not a purely academic text in its strictest sense.

The weaving clusters that are a focus of this study are Phulia village in the Nadia district of West Bengal, Bhujodi village in the Kutch district of Gujarat and Kuthampully village in the Thrissur district of Kerala. The regions chosen for this study were selected purposefully, in part driven by different environmental zones, not just in terms of ecological systems and monsoon patterns but also the polarities of climate that affect them, from extreme humidity to extreme dryness and wetness. I was looking at how each of these weather elements directly or indirectly impacted the making of the textile. Additionally, all three regions, for the most part of history, have witnessed repeated calamities – famines in Bengal, earthquakes in Kutch and floods in Kerala. Coincidentally, this selection of geographies also aligns with how the regions of Gujarat in Western India, Coromandel in Southern India and later Bengal in the East were among the most thriving centres of manufacturing within the international trade exchange of the eighteenth century.[29] Connections can be drawn down to present times as well – cotton slivers are sourced from Thrissur to spinning centres in Bengal while on the other hand *gamchhas,* woven by women of Tantipara in West Bengal are sent for sale in Kerala.[30] Not just woven textiles but a large number of male population out migrate from West Bengal to Kerala for better wages.

Simultaneously functioning as both a living and a working space, the weaving areas were often congested, dimly lit and not very well-ventilated. The language of a space is as different as the spoken language, as anthropologist Edward T. Hall posits in his book *The Hidden Dimension*.[31] There were exceptions in all three regions where houses were modernised and well-organised with clearly demarcated spaces for work and living. On the other hand, there was a house in Babla village in the Nadia district, where the entire space within was taken over by the loom; the loom accommodated the room instead of the other way around. Such cases of extreme privations were not far and few between. The field visits left me with a deep appreciation for the bodily labour that weavers engage in daily. As a mere visitor in their spaces, I found the weather and at places the din of power looms unbearable, particularly in the numbing humidity of Bengal and in the blinding heat of Kutch. I could only imagine how it is for the weavers to work day in and out, stretching yarn and hours on the looms.

Chapter 2 'The Indian Weaver through History' charts the story of the Indian weaver through recorded history and how changes in climate have altered the craft and traditional processes. Chapter 3 'Migration and the Indian Weaver' uncovers stories of weavers' historical and contemporary migration, zooming in on the three weaving clusters. Stressing on women-centric narratives, Chapter 4 'Women, Weaving and Climate Change' decentres the image of the weaver as a man, focusing on women's contributions to the weaving activities that always cumulatively exceed the time a male weaver spends on the loom in a day.

Forming the first case study, Chapter 5 'Loom(ing) Hierarchies in Nadia' discusses how the making of Bengal muslin involved the continuous engagement of bodies, plants, monsoon and local materials. The chapter expands on how the ecology of this region is governed by hierarchies among the weaver settlements of Phulia and Santipur. The second case study, Chapter 6 'Weaving Indigenous Wisdom in Kutch' situates itself in the arid landscape of Western India. Bhujodi is a weaving village that continues its traditional weaving practices of working on pit looms and crafting textiles using desi oon. Where excessive warming is a relatively new phenomenon in many parts of the country, what can more dry heat do to an already broiling topography, the chapter builds this strand further. The third case study, Chapter 7 'The Kasavu Textiles of Kuthampully Handloom Village' goes down south to a village that weaves Kasavu saris. Positioned in a location that witnesses the confluence of two major rivers, the Devanga community of weavers here are erstwhile migrant weavers from Karnataka.

Approaches and Methods

While in Kutch, I spent time with wizened old men, in Bengal I pursued women who were busy performing chores around the house. The questions I had enlisted were not fixed for each interviewee but rather relied on the relationship I built with the weaver and their families in my initial conversations. Asking questions was not easy either; my interviewees had no ready answers. When asked if the changing climate over the years has impacted their weaving practices, the first answer was always in denial and there were no direct answers. In my conversations with the weavers, there surfaced a constant dichotomy where they would say that climate change has not impacted them much but as the discussion developed, they would share the changes they had noticed and felt.

At other times, it became difficult for me to articulate the subject of my research. Most of the informants were not aware of climate change and this was something I had expected too. So, I used the materials, processes, the ecology as a reference to frame my questions. I started with a discussion of their context and surroundings and any observable changes that the inhabitants had perceived. My queries were peppered with plenty of whys and hows and so the research is mostly a collection of these listenings and observations, collating and piecing together what I saw, heard and read.

In line with their slow pace of work, I was not rushing with my questions. The conversations allowed contemplation on the part of the interviewees and at times I took in silence as answers to my probing questions. Over several cups of sugary tea, at times sharing meals, cultivating patience for my curiosity became important. Lastly, while navigating the various spaces, I was sensitive to the geographies I was mapping and was mindful of the diverse social contexts of these spaces that I was wilfully entering. I was cautious of various social norms and mores, for instance, a young man in Nadia, one of my informants, could not be seen in public spaces walking in the company of two women – me and my friend.

Why this Book?

What started as marginalia on one of the pages of a key text, has now evolved into a project spanning three geographies. The research is an attempt to record weaving communities' lived and embodied experiences of climate change. As a qualitative appraisal of the effects of climate change faced by the weaving communities, what I am essentially doing is looking at tensions and forging connections through what I listened to and observed. Because the weavers themselves are less cognisant of how the changing climate is linked to their craft practice and what dangers it may pose for the future, the research will assist in channelling better support for Indian weavers. What I intend to do is bring to the forefront a diverse set of voices, from weavers and allied workers in the handloom industry, sharing their experiences with the changing climate.

The subject of my research transcends disciplines, fusing the two research strands of climate change and the craft of weaving. While handloom as a cottage industry has been a subject of much interest and so has climate change and its impact on the Global South, the two together have received a short shrift within existing scholarship. In a way, I am conjoining two different facets of looking at a crisis – a textile-focused and an environmental one, while also engaging with discourses of traditional knowledge and wisdom, weaving and spirituality, movement and migration and more. I attempt to break down the behemoth concept of climate change, from a complex, abstract entity to a perceptive experience of how it is felt in the everyday. In disambiguating the subject, the book shifts the focus from craft to craftswomen and craftsmen, from weaving to the weaver.

Climate change is omnipresent and ever-pervasive, yet it takes a perceptive and a perceptual observer to unravel the finer nuances. Craftspeople are ecologically sound and how they witness climate change and experience these epiphenomenon are important to record. It demands an attentiveness to the surrounding environment and in attending critically to these aspects, craftspeople become knowledge holders. Throughout the research for this book, I was regularly cautioning myself about how change is inevitable, it may or may not have the change in climate as a root cause. I am thus conscious of the idea of 'climate reductionism' which geographer Mike Hulme specifically warns against.[32] I am also conscious of my positionality, echoing environmentalist Ashish Kothari's comment, "Why someone who writes about organic farmers is paid more than the organic farmer [himself]?"[33]. The topicality of climate change as a research subject has not escaped me and also why one must caution against it.

Weaving historian Prasannan Parthasarathi's notable text on how weavers and handloom industry suffered in the face of famines, ridiculous colonial policies and imports contains a brief mention of climate change and its continuing influence in the present times.[34] Scholarship exists on the rising effects of climate change in India, the importance of soil and water bodies in agriculture and weaving, Indian weaving history, the economy of the weaving industry, weavers and migration, and craft and sustainability.[35] However, there is limited literature available that discusses relationships between craft and climate change and almost negligible on climate change adaptation in the context of weavers.

Echoing historian Murari Jha's words, several texts study the weavers in the Coromandel Coast or broadly South India, however, there are relatively few that focus on weavers in Bengal or Gujarat and these have remained peripheral in the existing scholarship.[36] Also, across historical texts that have studied weavers in South India, modern Kerala is often not included since no cotton cultivation took place in the region and there was little textile production.[37]

This book engages with an urgent contemporary issue, that puts centre stage voices from the weavers. By tracing this traditional knowledge that resides with the weavers, of processes and practices, of changing climate and how it results in a shift in seasonal patterns, the book plugs a critical gap. What is even sparsely recorded are weavers' lived realities of climate change, experiences that cannot be homogenised. The book thus breaks away from the monolithic experiences of the weavers while interacting with the changing climate.

Crafts have fairly remained delinked from the subject of climate science or the larger issue of climate change. Voicing the effects will compel people from other disciplines to acknowledge the subtleties and engage below the surface. It will help translate the abstract conversations around climate change to the shifts happening on the ground with weavers and their livelihoods. Not only climate change forms one of the most pressing issues of our times but its complex representation further makes it difficult for people to discern the underlying causes and how it affects on an individual level, particularly the ones pushed to the periphery. It is also important to dismantle the idea of climate change as understood in the West and instead bring in an understanding of lesser-recognised concepts such as traditional climate knowledge and the gendered effects of climate change.

While I had set out to map the effects of the changing climate on weaving, the research revealed insights into the precarity of the handloom industry in India and how the next decade is crucial for its sustenance. Witnessing deserted looms in Phulia village with the warp still intact on the loom, a sari left suspended in its making or looms dissolving in the sands of the desert in Varnora village in Kutch or the foliage taking over a deserted production shed in Devangapuram in Kerala – these scenes of dilapidation were evocative of the industry being at the cusp, of times changing, of an era where handloom may soon become an exotic vision rather than an everyday craft. The decrepit state of these settings, the closing on of pits in Kuthampully village coupled with the pulsating sounds of power looms in the weaving village of Nadia were sounding like a death knell instead.

In attempting to form associations between climate change and weaving practices, the new knowledge will help generate support for Indian weavers. Handloom weaving continues to form an intrinsic part of the rural and local economy in India; many craftspeople still sell in both rural and urban haats. Acting as a valuable resource to scholars of policy, development, economy, cultural ecology, craft researchers, and design historians, the foundational discussions in the book will help cultivate further conversations.

Notes

1 Eric Broudy, *The Book of Looms: A History of the Handloom from Ancient Times to the Present* (UK, Hanover: University Press of New England, 1993), 13–14.
2 Peru is another region where weaving developed alongside. See Broudy, *The Book of Looms*, 50.
3 The exact number is 2,37,700 looms. See "Handloom Sector in India," ClearIAS, last modified February 15, 2024, https://www.clearias.com/handloom-sector-india/.
4 Uzramma, "The Indian Loom, Climate Change, and Democracy: Introducing the Malkha Enterprise," *Comparative Studies of South Asia, Africa and the Middle East* 39, no. 2 (August 2019): 233–240.
5 Weaving was categorically part of the 'village industries' during the Swaraj (self-sufficiency) movement of the early twentieth century, propelled by Mahatma Gandhi.
6 Ramaswamy writes how this 'polarization' of weavers' roles has existed since the late medieval period. See Vijaya Ramaswamy, "The Genesis and Historical Role of the Masterweavers in South Indian Textile Production," *Journal of the Economic and Social History of the Orient* 28, no. 3 (1985): 294–325.
7 Prasannan Parthasarathi, *The Transition to a Colonial Economy: Weavers, Merchants and Kings in South India, 1720–1800*. No. 7. (Cambridge: Cambridge University Press, 2001).
8 Aruna Bagchee, "Vernacular Architecture of Handloom Sari Weavers in India: A Case for Conservation of Traditional Houses and Settlements of Handloom Weavers' Clusters," *Journal of Heritage Management* 3, no. 1 (2018): 1–26.
9 M. Saiful Islam, *Muslin! Our Story* (Drik Picture Library, 2016).
10 Parthasarathi, *Transition to Colonial Economy*, 6.
11 Gyanendra Pandey, "The Bigoted Julaha," *Economic and Political Weekly* (January 1983): 19–28.

12 Sandip Hazareesingh, "Cotton, Climate and Colonialism in Dharwar, Western India, 1840–1880," *Journal of Historical Geography* 38, no. 1 (2012): 1–17.
13 For the larger context, see Case Study 2 in Chapter 7.
14 Debashre Mukherjee, "Cotton Weaving Industry of Nadia 1773–1977: A Case Study of Santipur and Phulia," PhD diss., (University of North Bengal, 2011).
15 Sushma Iyengar, "Reviving a Heritage in Peril: India's Endangered Traditions of Cotton and Wool," *Journal of Heritage Management* 6, no. 1 (Month 2021): 25–39.
16 Uzramma, "The Indian Loom, Climate Change, and Democracy".
17 Henry Yule and Arthur Coke Burnell, *Hobson-Jobson: A Glossary of Colloquial Anglo-Indian Words and Phrases, and of Kindred Terms, Etymological, Historical, Geographical and Discursive* (London: John Murray, 1903).
18 See Margaret Bruchac, "Indigenous Knowledge and Traditional Knowledge," *Encyclopaedia of Global Archaeology* 10 (2014): 3814–3824.
19 Vijaya Ramaswamy, "Alien Weave: Crafts Verses Consumerism," *India International Centre Quarterly* 29, no. 2 (2002): 117–128.
20 Tim Ingold, *Correspondences* (Cambridge: Polity Press, 2021).
21 However, the earliest weaving used to take place under the open sky. See Broudy, *The Book of Looms*, 106.
22 Clifford Geertz, "Art as a Cultural System," *mln* 91, no. 6 (December 1976): 1473–1499.
23 Glenn Adamson, *The Invention of Craft* (London: Bloomsbury Academic/V&A Publishing, 2013), xiii.
24 Dipaka Maheta, *Work, Ritual, Biography: A Muslim Community in North India* (Delhi: Oxford University Press, 1997), 74.
25 For a detailed discussion on the history of the 'Indian Loom', see Broudy, *The Book of Looms*, 10.
26 Broudy, *The Book of Looms*, 54.
27 Hailing from Mysore in Karnataka, the Devanga community in Kuthampully speaks Kannada as their mother tongue. However, they are conversant with Malayalam too, since they were born and raised in Kerala.
28 This research project was entirely self-funded.
29 Giorgio Riello and Tirthankar Roy, *How India Clothed the World: The World of South Asian Textiles, 1500–1850 (Volume 4)* (Leiden; Boston: Brill, 2009), 1.
30 Archana Shah, *Crafting a Future: Stories of Indian Textiles and Sustainable Practices* (New Delhi: Niyogi Books, 2021).
31 Edward T. Hall, *The Hidden Dimension* (New York: Anchor Books, 1982), xii.
32 Mike Hulme, "Reducing the Future to Climate: A Story of Climate Determinism and Reductionism," *Osiris* 26, no. 1 (2011): 245–266.
33 Ashish Kothari, *Eco-Swaraj: Pluriversal Pathways out of Global Crises* (Zoom Webinar, Centre De Sciences Humanities, September 4, 2023).

34 Parthasarathi, *Transition to Colonial Economy*.
35 Navroz K. Dubash, ed., *India in a Warming World: Integrating Climate Change and Development* (New Delhi: Oxford University Press, 2019); Lyla Mehta, Hans Nicolai Adam, and Shilpi Srivastava, *The Politics of Climate Change and Uncertainty in India* (New York: Routledge, 2022); Meena Menon and Uzramma, *A Frayed History: The Journey of Cotton in India* (New Delhi: Oxford University Press, 2017); Giorgio Riello, *Cotton: The Fabric that Made the Modern World* (New York: Cambridge University Press, 2013); Vandana Shiva, "Women's Indigenous Knowledge and Biodiversity Conservation," *India International Centre Quarterly* 19, no. 1/2 (1992): 205–214; Parthasarathi, *Transition to Colonial Economy*; Vijaya Ramaswamy, *Textiles and Weavers in Medieval South India* (OUP, 2006); Soumhya Venkatesan, *Craft Matters: Artisans, Development and the Indian Nation* (Orient Blackswan Private Limited, 2009); Douglas E. Haynes, *Small Town Capitalism in Western India: Artisans, Merchants, and the Making of the Informal Economy, 1870–1960*. No. 20 (New York: Cambridge University Press, 2012); Abigail McGowan, *Crafting the Nation in Colonial India* (New York: Palgrave Macmillan, 2009); Tirthankar Roy, *The Crafts and Capitalism: Handloom Weaving industry in Colonial India* (New York: Routledge, 2020); Geraldine Terry, *Climate Change and Gender Justice* (UK: Practical Action Publishing, 2009).
36 Murari Jha, "Weavers in early modern South Asia (Sixteenth–Seventeenth Centuries)," in *The Indian Ocean in the Making of Early Modern India*, ed. Pius Malekandathil (UK: Routledge, 2017), 291–327.
37 See Parthasarathi, *Transition to Colonial Economy*, 7.

Bibliography

Adamson, Glenn. *The Invention of Craft*. London: Bloomsbury Academic/V&A Publishing, 2013.

Bagchee, Aruna. "Vernacular Architecture of Handloom Sari Weavers in India: A Case for Conservation of Traditional Houses and Settlements of Handloom Weavers' Clusters." *Journal of Heritage Management* 3, no. 1 (2018): 1–26.

Broudy, Eric. *The Book of Looms: A History of the Handloom from Ancient Times to the Present*. UK, Hanover: University Press of New England, 1993.

Bruchac, Margaret. "Indigenous Knowledge and Traditional Knowledge." *Encyclopaedia of Global Archaeology* 10 (2014): 3814–3824.

Dubash, Navroz K. ed. *India in a Warming World: Integrating Climate Change and Development*. New Delhi: Oxford University Press, 2019.

Geertz, Clifford. "Art as a Cultural System." *mln* 91, no. 6 (December 1976): 1473–1499.

Hall, Edward T. *The Hidden Dimension*. New York: Anchor Books, 1982.

Hazareesingh, Sandip. "Cotton, Climate and Colonialism in Dharwar, Western India, 1840–1880." *Journal of Historical Geography* 38, no. 1 (2012): 1–17.

Haynes, Douglas E. *Small Town Capitalism in Western India: Artisans, Merchants, and the Making of the Informal Economy, 1870–1960*. No. 20. New York: Cambridge University Press, 2012.

Hulme, Mike. "Reducing the Future to Climate: A Story of Climate Determinism and Reductionism." *Osiris* 26, no. 1 (2011): 245–266.

Ingold, Tim. *Correspondences*. Cambridge: Polity Press, 2021.

Islam, M. Saiful. *Muslin! Our Story*. Drik Picture Library, 2016.

Iyengar, Sushma. "Reviving a Heritage in Peril: India's Endangered Traditions of Cotton and Wool." *Journal of Heritage Management* 6, no. 1 (Month 2021): 25–39.

Jha, Murari. "Weavers in Early Modern South Asia (Sixteenth–Seventeenth Centuries)." In *The Indian Ocean in the Making of Early Modern India*, edited by Pius Malekandathil, 291–327. UK: Routledge, 2017.

Kothari, Ashish. "Eco-Swaraj: Pluriversal Pathways out of Global Crises." Zoom Webinar. Centre De Sciences Humanities, September 4, 2023. https://www.youtube.com/watch?v=4vk8fnu29YA.

McGowan, Abigail. *Crafting the Nation in Colonial India*. New York: Palgrave Macmillan, 2009.

Maheta, Dipaka. *Work, Ritual, Biography: A Muslim Community in North India*. Delhi: Oxford University Press, 1997.

Mehta, Lyla, Hans Nicolai Adam and Shilpi Srivastava. *The Politics of Climate Change and Uncertainty in India*. New York: Routledge, 2022.

Menon, Meena and Uzramma. *A Frayed History: The Journey of Cotton in India*. New Delhi: Oxford University Press, 2017.

Mukherjee, Debashre. "Cotton Weaving Industry of Nadia 1773–1977: A Case Study of Santipur and Phulia." PhD diss., University of North Bengal, 2011.

Pandey, Gyanendra. "The Bigoted Julaha." *Economic and Political Weekly* (January 1983): 19–28.

Parthasarathi, Prasannan. *The Transition to a Colonial Economy: Weavers, Merchants and Kings in South India, 1720–1800*. No. 7. Cambridge: Cambridge University Press, 2001.

Ramaswamy, Vijaya. "The Genesis and Historical Role of the Masterweavers in South Indian Textile Production." *Journal of the Economic and Social History of the Orient* 28, no. 3 (1985): 294–325.

Ramaswamy, Vijaya. "Alien Weave: Crafts Verses Consumerism." *India International Centre Quarterly* 29, no. 2 (2002): 117–128.

Ramaswamy, Vijaya. *Textiles and Weavers in Medieval South India*. OUP, 2006.

Riello, Giorgio. *Cotton: The Fabric that Made the Modern World*. New York: Cambridge University Press, 2013.

Riello, Giorgio and Tirthankar Roy. *How India Clothed the World: The World of South Asian Textiles, 1500–1850 (Volume 4)*. Leiden, Boston: Brill, 2009.

Roy, Tirthankar. *The Crafts and Capitalism: Handloom Weaving Industry in Colonial India*. New York: Routledge, 2020.

Shah, Archana. *Crafting a Future: Stories of Indian Textiles and Sustainable Practices*. New Delhi: Niyogi Books, 2021.

Shiva, Vandana. "Women's Indigenous Knowledge and Biodiversity Conservation." *India International Centre Quarterly* 19, no. 1/2 (1992): 205–214.

Terry, Geraldine. *Climate Change and Gender Justice*. UK: Practical Action Publishing, 2009.

Uzramma. "The Indian Loom, Climate Change, and Democracy: Introducing the Malkha Enterprise." *Comparative Studies of South Asia, Africa and the Middle East* 39, no. 2 (August 2019): 233–240.

Venkatesan, Soumhya. *Craft Matters: Artisans, Development and the Indian Nation*. Orient Blackswan Private Limited, 2009.

Yule, Henry and Arthur Coke Burnell. *Hobson-Jobson: A Glossary of Colloquial Anglo-Indian Words and Phrases, and of Kindred Terms, Etymological, Historical, Geographical and Discursive*. London: John Murray, 1903.

2 The Indian Weaver through History

The handloom industry in India traces its origins to as early as the oldest civilisations – Harappans were considered world pioneers in weaving and spinning.[1] Looking further back, in the Vedic times, the weaving of cloth symbolised the cosmos, with the weaver bestowed with the status of the 'Creator', one who creates cloth for various landmarks in life.[2]

Tanti, *Bunkar*, *Julaha* – irrespective of the part of the country the weaver works from, weaving was (and still is) a part of one's social and communal identity.[3] In an agrarian economy like India's, weaving has always formed an important subsistence occupation. As an erstwhile caste-based profession, weaving has been carried out since *satyug* – Sant Kabir was a weaver and so were Tulsidas and Ravidas Mahatma, earlier a shoemaker and a leatherworker respectively.[4] It was only with the Mughal intervention, their patronage that spurred the establishment of various *karkhanas* (workshops) and subsequent development of weaving clusters across the country that handloom gained its prestige. However, the tyrannical policies of the East India Company in later centuries led to its slow cessation.

Briefly looking at the Indian weaver through history, the chapter draws into focus the nineteenth and twentieth centuries when the build-up of the warming as we know it today, was in its initial phase. The discussion will situate the Indian weaver within the broader context of the impact of recurring famines, droughts and other ecological calamities as well as traditional cotton growing practices and strident colonial policies of the Raj, and how these eventually impacted the many cultures of weaving across the country, with a focus on the three clusters.

As mentioned in the Introduction section too, there is more to weaving beyond the act of interlacing on the loom as the final stage, a stage that has been privileged while discussing handwoven textiles. What is generally left out of the discussion are various pre-loom and post-loom processes such as cotton picking, ginning, cleaning, carding, slivering, spinning, sizing, dyeing, warping, beaming, washing, finishing and folding operations. I want to borrow here Annapurna Mamidipudi's idea of handloom as a

DOI: 10.4324/9781003450061-2

'sociotechnical ensemble of weaving'.[5] She writes that the term 'handloom' encapsulates the elements and tools involved before the yarn arrives at the weaving stage which includes charkhas, looms, warping drums as well as practices of sizing and designing including computerised work, various institutions such as households, weaving communities and other ancillary workers. While weaving has always received much scholarly attention, the processes built around this main activity, which constitute equally a part of the weaver's 'craft knowledge', have received little focus.[6]

In terms of spaces, while earlier all the processes used to take place in-house, the systems have disaggregated now. The yarn used to be hand-spun by women at home and available to the weavers as hanks. Now, ready-made mill-spun yarn is retailed as cones, purchased by the weavers from the nearest market. Most of the processes stated above have been mechanised in present times or a chemical substitute has replaced a natural raw material. For instance, sizing, a process used to starch the warp yarns to achieve an even weave on the loom, was earlier done with a solution of *khoi*—a mixture of parched rice, sago starch and neem oil or a mixture of ragi (a millet variety) and tamarind powder—which has now been replaced with starch powder.

The weaver who used to wax lyrical about his wealth of knowledge of natural dyes, synthetic dyes have now become commonplace owing to the ease of process, ready availability and accessibility. The use of such dyes has had an irreversible impact on traditional Indian practices as well as the surrounding environment in which the weavers operate. Another problematic intervention has been the selective replacement of the handloom with a power loom. For instance, villages in the Nadia district in Bengal are dotted with power looms but none could be spotted in the villages of Kutch or in Kuthampully in Kerala. As was revealed, it is not that people cannot afford to get a power loom installed in these regions, but the production will be in such numbers that the stock will be unmanageable for the weaver, let alone sell it. Large production requires a large customer base too and if there is plenty of inventory, individual prices of the products will eventually plummet.[7]

The Weaver Who Persevered

The handloom workers have been subjected to repeated adversities for over a century now, beginning with the yarn crisis during the Second World War that resulted in increased taxation, inflation and other harsher policies imposed by the British government, to the more recent starvation deaths in villages around Chirala in Andhra Pradesh in 1991 due to a sudden surge in the price of cotton yarn. Weavers have always been known to adapt and negotiate when their environment changes, but they remain disempowered. Referred to as 'history's largest socio-economic tragedy', suicide cases among cotton farmers were once rampant, particularly, in the cotton-growing state of Maharashtra.[8] Weaver suicides reached their peak in 2001, in a post-liberalised India. The use of chemical dyes further pushed many to the brink.[9] With unequal access to resources and markets, the changing climate seems to have further worsened their plight. The introduction of the power loom did not make the situation any better as is evidenced by a steep rise in the number of power loom operator suicides being recorded.[10] A series of policy decisions and ground realities of the handloom sector are deemed responsible for this catastrophe.

The weaver as a craftsperson has been equally valorised and pauperised throughout history. The slow decline that the sector began in colonial India has continued its trajectory despite the efforts to 'revive' and 'sustain' the industry. Some historians offer a countervailing view by arguing how there was a rise in handloom in the first half of the twentieth century, compared to a drastic decline in the nineteenth century.[11] However, it later faced several setbacks including outmoded technology, unorganised production, market alterations, social and economic vulnerabilities and a risk to other interrelationships. It was the 2020 pandemic-induced lockdown where the sector received another blow with millions walking back home, either forcibly or voluntarily.[12] With many weavers retrenched, the lockdown impacted their already precarious livelihoods and daily subsistence.

The Weaver's Looms

Across the country, one may witness a variety of looms, depending on the climate, geographies as well as diverse weaving cultures. Similarly, an array of looms was encountered in all the three regions involved in this study. Alexander Langlands in his book *Craeft* discusses vernacular tool types, on how the part of the country one comes from influences the shape of the tool.[13] The traditional pit looms are the earliest treadle looms known to have existed in India.[14] As the name suggests, a pit is dug in the ground, usually two feet deep with enough space for the weaver's legs to press the treadle. The finest cotton and silks were produced on these looms because the pit facilitated humidity and moisture which was ideal for weaving these fibres.[15] The moisture offered by the pit loom, proves to be an advantage in the dry season, as it obviates any breakage of the warp threads. Even now most of the floors in weavers' homes are comprised of undulating wet earth instead of evenly flattened concrete.[16] Because of the limited raw material required in its construction, the pit loom was well-suited to an environment with little wood as a resource. This rudimentary construction of the loom was also congruent with the nature of the weaver which was essentially itinerant in the past.

When weavers were asked how they started weaving on the pit loom in the first place, *parampara* (tradition) was often rallied as an answer – generations have done this way, so they do it too. While in Kutch, the pit loom structure has rarely changed, in Kuthampully, the majority of the looms are now fitted with a jacquard box on top that makes for a piece of a traditional-modern weaving equipment. Raised from the ground up at a certain height, the stand or table loom shares less contact with the earth. Although the stand looms have now become the most visible looms across India, they still differ in every region in terms of dimension, material, height and other variables that best suit a weaver's ergonomics of work.

Undertaken beneath covered areas, most weavers had looms as part of their homes or as a detached room in the same courtyard. However, weaving in enclosed or semi-covered structures is a recent development, there was a time when it was performed in the open air. Historian James Mill discusses in *The History of India*, how the house of the weaver is not sufficient to 'contain' him and therefore, he is compelled to work in the open air with every return of 'inclement weather' interrupting his work.[17]

With a portion of the loom lying beneath the ground, a pit loom is also, a weaver's favoured choice when compared to other loom types, because it is better spatialised by providing ample space in the weaving area to be utilised for another loom or for carrying out any weaving-related process or to store materials. This preference, however, varies across regions, for instance, in Kuthampully, where space holds a different meaning, a stand loom is considered more spatialised. In a village that has many migrant weavers who stay in one-room tenements, a loom raised from the ground allows space for the weaver to sleep underneath – the loom becomes the weaver's home.[18] Both pit loom and stand loom can either have the arrangement of a throw shuttle (which entails manually passing of the warp threads) or a fly shuttle (using a pull-rope kind of mechanism, which drastically increases the production pace). In many cases, the yarn informs the loom use and vice versa, for instance, in some areas, the traditional shuttle has been replaced with a fly shuttle because the latter is suitable for mill-spun yarn which has now increasingly replaced hand-spun yarn. This has been a regular feature across handloom weaving clusters in India.

Climate Changes, Weaving Changes

Eighteenth-century onwards, the Indian handloom industry started its slow decline, witnessing a 'secular deterioration' in climatic conditions.[19] Weavers first suffered when the disintegration of the political regime took place as the Mughal Empire loosened its grip. This led to a slump in agricultural productivity that subsequently created an erratic supply of raw materials, thereby affecting cloth manufacture.[20] This was further aggravated by extreme changes in climatic conditions leading to regular droughts – nearly one every two years and these continued for the better part of the eighteenth and nineteenth centuries.[21] . This phenomenon of 'deindustrialisation' of India that defined the decline of the handloom industry during this time has remained of much interest to many historians.[22] Soon, middlemen entered the market, thereby monopolising the sector. In fact, these middlemen were the ones to be blamed by the colonial officials for the weavers' economic hardship.[23]

As per scholars who expound on the 'deindustrialisation' theory, the primary cause was the surge in textile manufacturing industries in Britain that gave tough competition to Indian handloom. Another reason was the opening of alternative trade routes that offered better connectivity and facilitated increased transcontinental trade. Some historians also contend that it was the climate, as one of the important factors, that aided this international trade. However, this very climate impacted the trade with the influence of monsoon winds in setting the rhythm of production and exports in the Indian Ocean region and then a drop in the winds, nineteenth century onwards.[24] But this was also the quarter (1900–1925) that saw recurrent famines in India and the colonial regime further worsened the situation.

There are multiple narratives as to how this systemic collapse unravelled itself – the image of skilled weavers having their fingers chopped off has repeatedly been reproduced as an evocative metaphor of their plight. Poulomi Saha in *An Empire of Touch* argues how "the body of the artisans did not render the cloth valuable; rather, its value obscured the body that laboured in its production."[25] The weaver slowly metamorphosed from an 'independent' weaver to a 'dependent' weaver.[26] This has strongly been reflected in the case of Nadia district in Bengal, where the weaver has transitioned from a seller of cloth to a seller of labour.[27]

In the early twentieth century, as part of Gandhian politics, handwoven cloth assumed a different significance. The century thus witnessed an 'urbanization of artisanal cloth production', with weaving becoming focused in a few pockets, unlike an everyday practice.[28] Historian Douglas E. Haynes attributes this shift to the migration of artisans from other parts of India.[29] In the early nineteenth century, as part of Gandhian politics, handwoven cloth assumed a different significance.[30] In later decades, there was also the proliferation of 'weaver-capitalists' or 'entrepreneur weaver-capitalists' who were scaling up workshops and incorporating the most recent technological changes, by purchasing power looms in their homes or by constructing weaving sheds.[31] This can be considered the forerunner of the present-day power loom industry that has transmuted into the most important form of industrial employment in India.

Notes

1 John Keay, *India: A History* (India: Harper Collins, 2010).
2 Bela Sanghvi, *The Mystery of Patola: The Fabric that is Forever* (Zoom Webinar, Bangalore International Centre, October 18, 2021).
3 These are the various names that denote a weaver across regions in India.
4 Bhamal Jaimalji, personal communication, January 5, 2024.
5 Annapurna Mamidipudi, "Towards a Theory of Innovation in Handloom Weaving in India," (2016).
6 I borrow this term from Dormer. See Peter Dormer, *The Art of the Maker: Skill and its Meaning in Art, Craft and Design* (London: Thames & Hudson, 1994).
7 Hamirji Vishram, personal communication, January 1, 2024.
8 Uzramma, "The Indian Loom, Climate Change, and Democracy: Introducing the Malkha Enterprise," *Comparative Studies of South Asia, Africa and the Middle East* 39, no. 2 (August 2019): 233–240.
9 For a detailed account of weavers' struggle, see K. Srinivasulu, "Handloom Weavers' Struggle for Survival," *Economic and Political Weekly* (September 1994): 2331–2333.
10 "Weaver Ends Life; Sixth Suicide in Last 10 Days". *Indian Express*, January 9, 2015. https://www.newindianexpress.com/states/telangana/2015/Jan/09/weaver-ends-life-sixth-suicide-in-last-10-days-703108.html.
11 Tirthankar Roy, "Relations of Production in Handloom Weaving in the Mid-1930s," Economic and Political Weekly (1989): PE-21–PE-34.
12 I wrote a poem about this during the 2020 lockdown. See Pragya Sharma, "A Place Called Home," *Gulmohur Quarterly* 1 (March 2021).
13 Alexander Langlands, *Craeft: An Enquiry into the Origins and True Meaning of Traditional Crafts* (New York: Norton, 2018), 117.
14 The antecedents to the pit loom would have been the weaver suspending the harnesses from the branch of a tree under which a pit was dug to contain his legs and the treadles of the loom. See Eric Broudy, *The Book of Looms: A History of the Handloom from Ancient Times to the Present* (UK, Hanover: University Press of New England, 1993), 273.
15 Trilokanath Bose, *Bunai Aur Rangai* (1939).
16 Niloy Das, personal communication, July 11, 2023.
17 James Mill, *The History of British India*, Vol. I (London: Piper, Stephenson and Spence, 1858).
18 I thank Prof Saumya Pande for this insight.
19 David Clingingsmith and Jeffrey G. Williamson, "Mughal Decline, Climate Change, and Britain's Industrial Ascent: An Integrated Perspective on India's 18th and 19th Century Deindustrialization," (November 2005): 1.

20 For a detailed discussion on the connection between the Mughal Empire's collapse and the subsequent rise of British rule in India and how these events affected the textile industry, see Clingingsmith & Williamson, "Mughal Decline, Climate Change". There exists a parallel theory as well that the climatic events of the early eighteenth century were responsible for the fall of the Mughal Empire, see Richard H. Grove and John Chappell, eds., *El Niño-history and Crisis Studies from Asia-Pacific Region* (Cambridge: White Horse Press, 2000), 15.

21 See the work of climate historians including Richard H. Grove, *Ecology, Climate and Empire: Colonialism and Global Environmental History, 1400–1940* (Cambridge: White Horse Press, 1997); Grove and Chappell, eds. *El Niño-History*; Richard Grove, Vinita Damodaran and Satpal Sangwan, eds. *Nature and the Orient: The Environmental History of South and South-East Asia* (New Delhi: Oxford University Press, 1998).

22 Amiya Kumar Bagchi, "De-industrialization in India in the Nineteenth Century: Some Theoretical Implications," *The Journal of Development Studies* 12, no. 2 (1976): 135–164; Peter Harnetty, "'Deindustrialization' Revisited: The Handloom Weavers of the Central Provinces of India, c. 1800–1947," *Modern Asian Studies* 25, no. 3 (July 1991): 455–510; Haynes, "Artisan Cloth-producers"; Indrajit Ray, "The Myth and Reality of Deindustrialisation in Early Modern India," *A New Economic History of Colonial India* (2015): 52–66; Colimn Simmons, "'De-industrialization', Industrialization and the Indian Economy, c. 1850–1947," *Modern Asian Studies* 19, no. 3 (April 1985): 593–622.

23 Leslie Hempson, "Colonial Weaving Schools and the New 'Middleman': United Provinces, India, 1905–1925," master's thesis, (University of North Carolina, 2011).

24 See Giorgio Riello and Tirthankar Roy, *How India Clothed the World: The World of South Asian Textiles, 1500–1850*. Vol. 4. (Leiden; Boston: Brill, 2009), 8.

25 Poulomi Saha, *An Empire of Touch: Women's Political Labor and the Fabrication of East Bengal* (New York: Columbia University Press, 2019), 111.

26 Roy, "Relations of Production".

27 A sentiment echoed in Roy's text as well. See Roy, "Relations of Production," PE-22.

28 Roy, "Relations of Production".

29 Douglas E.Haynes, "Artisan Cloth-producers and the Emergence of Powerloom Manufacture in Western India 1920–1950," *Past & Present* 172 (2001): 176.

30 Also see Christopher A. Bayly and Arjun Appadurai, *The Origins of Swadeshi (Home Industry): Cloth and Indian Society, 1700–1930* (Cambridge: Cambridge University Press, 1986); D.U. Sastry, "The Politics of Textiles: The Indian Cotton Mill Industry and the Legacy of Swadeshi" (December 1993): 261–263.

31 For a detailed discussion see Haynes, "Artisan Cloth-producers," 173; Roy 2017, 109–130.

Bibliography

Bagchi, Amiya Kumar. "De-industrialization in India in the Nineteenth Century: Some Theoretical Implications." *The Journal of Development Studies* 12, no. 2 (1976): 135–164.

Bayly, Christopher A. and Arjun Appadurai. *The Origins of Swadeshi (Home Industry): Cloth and Indian Society, 1700–1930*. Cambridge: Cambridge University Press, 1986.

Bose, Trilokanath. *Bunai Aur Rangai*. 1939.

Broudy, Eric. *The Book of Looms: A History of the Handloom from Ancient Times to the Present*. UK, Hanover: University Press of New England, 1993.

Clingingsmith, David and Jeffrey G. Williamson. "Mughal Decline, Climate Change, and Britain's Industrial Ascent: An Integrated Perspective on India's 18th and 19th Century Deindustrialization." (November 2005).

Dormer, Peter. *The Art of the Maker: Skill and its Meaning in Art, Craft and Design*. London: Thames & Hudson, 1994.

Grove, Richard H. *Ecology, Climate and Empire: Colonialism and Global Environmental History, 1400–1940*. Cambridge: White Horse Press, 1997.

Grove, Richard H. and John Chappell, eds. *El Niño-history and Crisis Studies from Asia-Pacific Region*. Cambridge: White Horse Press, 2000.

Grove, Richard, Vinita Damodaran and Satpal Sangwan, eds. *Nature and the Orient: The Environmental History of South and South-East Asia*. New Delhi: Oxford University Press, 1998.

Harnetty, Peter. "'Deindustrialization' Revisited: The Handloom Weavers of the Central Provinces of India, c. 1800–1947." *Modern Asian Studies* 25, no. 3 (July 1991): 455–510.

Haynes, Douglas E. "Artisan Cloth-producers and the Emergence of Powerloom Manufacture in Western India 1920–1950." *Past & Present* 172 (2001): 170–198.

Hempson, Leslie. "Colonial Weaving Schools and the New 'Middleman': United Provinces, India, 1905–1925." master's thesis, 2011.

Keay, John. *India: A History*. India: Harper Collins, 2010.

Langlands, Alexander. *Craeft: An Enquiry into the Origins and True Meaning of Traditional Crafts*. New York: Norton, 2018.

Mamidipudi, Annapurna. "Towards a Theory of Innovation in Handloom Weaving in India." (2016).

Mill, James. *The History of British India*. Vol. I. London: Piper, Stephenson and Spence, 1858.

Ray, Indrajit. "The Myth and Reality of Deindustrialisation in Early Modern India." *A New Economic History of Colonial India* (2015): 52–66.

Riello, Giorgio and Tirthankar Roy. *How India Clothed the World: The World of South Asian Textiles, 1500–1850*. Vol. 4. Leiden; Boston: Brill, 2009.

Roy, Tirthankar. "Relations of Production in Handloom Weaving in the Mid-1930s." *Economic and Political Weekly* (1989): PE21–PE34.

Saha, Poulomi. *An Empire of Touch: Women's Political Labor and the Fabrication of East Bengal.* New York: Columbia University Press, 2019.

Sanghvi, Bela. *The Mystery of Patola: The Fabric that is Forever*. Zoom Webinar. Bangalore International Centre, October 18, 2021. https://www.youtube.com/watch?v=HrL7FYh4Vac&t=1530s.

Sastry, D.U. "The Politics of Textiles: The Indian Cotton Mill Industry and the Legacy of Swadeshi." (December 1993): 261–263.

Sharma, Pragya. "A Place called Home." *Gulmohur Quarterly* 1 (March 2021).

Simmons, Colin. "'De-industrialization', Industrialization and the Indian Economy, c. 1850–1947." *Modern Asian Studies* 19, no. 3 (April 1985): 593–622.

Srinivasulu, K. "Handloom Weavers' Struggle for Survival." *Economic and Political Weekly* (September 1994): 2331–2333.

Uzramma. "The Indian Loom, Climate Change, and Democracy: Introducing the Malkha Enterprise." *Comparative Studies of South Asia, Africa and the Middle East* 39, no. 2 (August 2019): 233–240.

3 Migration and the Indian Weaver

Within the remit of South Asian history, weavers, among other people with distinctive craft skills, have been viewed as mobile.[1] Migration is considered one of the most common coping strategies (primarily for livelihood sustenance) adopted by the weavers in times of ecological crises, moving to cities or lands that hold better job prospects. However, migration for these weavers also results in what historian Vijaya Ramaswamy calls a 'dual alienation', from their habitat and their crafts.[2] This section will provide the reader with a brief historical overview of the weavers' movement and displacement across the country. For many, migration is not a choice but a matter of survival and not everyone can migrate as well, as Chinmay Tumbe reminds us in *India Moving*, how migration, other than human capital, requires physical, social, and financial capital too.[3] Other alternatives to migration include occupational change, conducting distress sales, borrowing money or material, reduced consumption or discontinuing the education of children. Lastly, the chapter will also discuss contemporary climate change-induced migrations of weavers.

The Itinerant Weaver in History

Recorded history propounds the narrative that the Hindu weaving caste group of Koshtis had migrated to Nagpur in Central India, in the mid-eighteenth century when the Maratha royal clan of Bhonsles established their ascendency as part of the Gond kingdom of Deogarh in Odisha.[4] In 1803, when famine hit the Deccan region, it induced weavers from Paithan, a silk-weaving centre on the Godavari, to come and settle in Nagpur at the invitation of the Raja of Nagpur.[5] Patnulkaran weavers of Saurashtra migrated from Gujarat in the West to Madurai in South India while Momins of Nagpur were immigrants from Mirzapur, a town on the Ganges near Varanasi in North India.[6]

DOI: 10.4324/9781003450061-3

In the East, Baluchari weavers in Murshidabad are supposedly weavers who migrated from Gujarat in the early eighteenth century.[7] In South India, weavers moved between Baramahal, Mysore and the Ceded Districts and this movement continued well into the eighteenth century. Devanga weavers, in the southern state of Kerala and Tamil Nadu, originally migrated from Mysore in Karnataka. Another important axis of migration was from Andhra to the Tamil country, which was part of a larger southward migration of Telugu-speaking peoples that began in the later medieval period.[8] These were just some of the journeys mapped by the weaving communities in India. It is often within the context of 'translocality', of having come from elsewhere, that binds these migrant communities together and this was visible in all three studied regions.[9]

The reasons to migrate differed across contexts. Wars and famines formed the two main reasons for the internal displacement of labour in the twentieth century.[10] At times, craftspeople were dislocated due to conflicts such as those caused by the wars with the Nawabs of Bengal in 1756–57 and 1763–65.[11] With British rule becoming entrenched in India, famines in Bengal became a regular occurrence. There was also a sudden paucity of female spinners as a result of famines in 1770 and then again during 1787–88, which reduced the quantity of fine yarn being produced, raising its price significantly.[12]

In the last five years, the Bengal region has been hit by four major cyclones, displacing inhabitants by thousands. Recently, the occupational shift has formed the most common reason why weavers migrate in search of a better livelihood. This mirrors the recent large-scale displacement of weavers in the aftermath of the COVID-19 pandemic. During my fieldwork in the three regions, I was greeted by idle, deserted looms, more often than I had expected to encounter; the weaver was on a prolonged absence. The following three sections offer detailed narratives of weavers' migration in Bengal, Kutch and Kerala.

Weavers on the Move in Nadia

The village of Phulia in Nadia district is a relatively new weaver settlement. Comprising of very few locals, 90% of the residents in Phulia belong to East Bengal.[13] With the 1947 partition of the subcontinent and subsequent migrations in 1965 and 1971, Phulia became a new cluster of Hindu migrant weavers who moved permanently from what was East Pakistan (present-day Bangladesh). Niloy Das, a PhD scholar at Visva-Bharati University at Santiniketan, refers to these weavers as 'transferred weavers' instead of using the term 'hereditary weavers'.[14]

Bangladesh today is still considered the original seat for the finest jamdani weaving. Poulomi Saha in *An Empire of Touch* elucidates this division of skill – how the Bengal partition was essentially an 'uncoupling of text from textile' where East Bengal continues to inherit the raw material and embodied labour.[15] Our caretaker in Phulia, Pranav Das, shared how his relatives are still residing in Bangladesh. He recounts the stories he has grown up hearing from his elders, of how when the partition of 1947 was announced, the migrants made the cross-border journey, from Bangladesh to India, with a bare sum in their pockets. *"Tant ke liye zameen nahi chhaiye"* (For a loom, one does not require much land), he says, asserting why setting up a loom was the most obvious choice for these migrants. Unlike farmers who need at least six *bhiga* land (a traditional unit of measuring land) to farm, weavers need only a small space to start with.[16]

The migrant weavers wove excellent saris, which generated good income, so they soon bought their own land and set up sari businesses which gave them great returns.[17] For the migrants, the craft of jamdani became their cultural imaginary. Jamdani saris woven in the Nadia district today are a testament to this shared textile history between India and Bangladesh. Because it is a migrant settlement, Phulia has a few Muslim weavers but not all of them are hereditary weavers. On the other hand, the ancient weaver settlement of Santipur (a 10-minute train ride from Phulia) has a predominantly Muslim population. During the partition, there were migrations from this side of the border as well, to Bangladesh.

"Migration is the most vital survival strategy", says biologist David Attenborough in the opening of the Netflix docuseries *Our Planet*.[18] Before the pandemic-induced lockdown of 2020, 700 weavers were active in Pranav's village, now only 100 are active.[19] The sari market vanished during the lockdown with the cost of weaving a sari decreasing considerably. The weaver was now being paid a mere amount of 120 INR per sari, where it was 180 INR earlier, for something that took him a day and a half. Three years after the first lockdown came into effect, the prices have still not recovered yet.

During the lockdown, many weavers who had previously migrated to Phulia had shut their loom sheds, left for their homes and have not returned since. Many have moved further up to Assam and are weaving textiles such as Mekhla chador.[20] Or they have moved to cities such as Delhi or far-off states such as Gujarat, Maharashtra or Kerala, working as construction labour and earning an average of 800 INR a day. Pranav is of the view that if somebody does not want to move out of Phulia or has no interest in studying, then one might choose to weave. It is distressing to come to terms with what weaving has come down to, from a craft passed on as a legacy to becoming the last resort for sustenance. The men who migrated out of Phulia now return every six months. In their place, women began learning to weave, even those who did not belong to the weaving community. They are from farmer or labour families but due to increased out-migration of male family members, they chose to learn to weave.

There are cases of temporary migrations as well where migrant workers travel within the state itself, from the Cooch Behar district in North Bengal to the Nadia district in the South. Although there are looms in their homelands but because the weaver gets paid more in Nadia, he is compelled to make the move, with his wages for weaving one sari seeing an increase, from 500 to 1000 INR.[21] Weaver families in Phulia are dependent on these migrant labourers; most looms are operated by them. Often, these weavers are classed as 'loom-less' weavers, signalling how strong the identity of the loom is attached to that of the weavers.' Apart from permanent and temporary migrations, there are circular migrations as well such as Pranav's father, an erstwhile weaver, who now works in Dubai and only gets to return every other year or so.

The Vankars of Kutch

How does one define a land traversed by a diversity of people at different points in time? Rita Kothari in *Memories and Movements* discusses Kutch as a region formed by multiple ethnicities, regions, and languages 'now coexisting, now coalescing'.[22] An erstwhile port city with active maritime trade, the region was well-connected in ancient and medieval India. These attributes helped foster in Kutch, what Kothari calls 'multi-raciality and hybridity' that still lingers in the region's air.[23] Kutch thus possesses a long history of migration where over the last 600 years, many migrant communities from Central Asia, Baluchistan, Afghanistan, Sindh, and Marwar, made this geography their home.[24] This makes Kutch a land of 'skilled immigrants' formed by centuries of migration incurred by droughts and famines, a search for fodder, trade, pilgrimage and political upheavals.[25]

Pastoralism, which once formed the primary occupation, had strong linkages with migration. Till about the 1970s, when borders were not so stringent, Banni pastoralists used to undertake seasonal migration between India and Pakistan, travelling from Kutch to Sindh and back again, all in a single day.[26] Their living was characterised by the temporary nature of their livelihoods. However, tight restrictions on the borders altered these migration patterns. The land is not the only resource lost to people when they are forcibly shifted; grazing grounds, fodder, herbs, forest produce and community labour, all of this goes away as well.[27]

Bhujodi in Kutch is not a very old settlement of weavers. Called Vankars, the weavers of Bhujodi traditionally belong to the Meghwal community. The introduction of weaving in Kutch can be traced back to 600 years ago when Meghwals migrated from Marwar in present-day Rajasthan, carrying their skill of weaving with them. Rabaris, a pastoralist community, for whom the Vankars used to originally weave, were also migrants from Marwar.

In present times, weavers in Kutch are considered more prosperous than others in the country. Their saris are considered expensive – from 500 INR for the price of a handwoven sari in Bengal to 5000 INR in Kutch. One of my interviewees in Varnora, another weaving village in Kutch, mentioned that the person who plays *manjira* (cymbals) as part of a *bhajan mandili* (a performing group of singers) gets paid 1000 INR rupees for 4–5 hours of playing. Contrarily, a weaver toiling away on his handloom in Bengal gets paid less![28] In a post-pandemic era, many weavers now retail online, maintain an active presence on social media and sell through channels such as WhatsApp and Instagram. They also share good visibility in craft fairs and bazaars such as Dastkar, Surajkund mela, Dastakari Haat Samiti and others across the country. Not just in India, weavers such as Naranbhai Siju, who has a carpet weaving set up in Bhujodi, have a huge market in Scandinavian countries with his signature aesthetic of undyed colours of black, white, brown and beige. In recent years, weavers from Kutch have shared spaces at annual events such as XTANT in Europe or International Folk Market Santa Fe in the United States.

Further, platforms such as Khamir with headquarters in Kukma village in Kutch, have helped many entrepreneur-weavers find a market. Following their suit, many other enterprises have entered the fray. All these aspects signal a promising future for Kutch propelling a wave of reverse migration in the region albeit with shifts in land ownership.[29] Where the entire land was once a part of the Commons, shared by various pastoralist communities, the government has now leased it to various industries. The setting up and functioning of these industries involve contractual labour which is either obtained from weavers-turned-labourers or brought in from outside of Kutch. This influx of people, apart from disrupting the social ecology of the region, has generated and widened social inequalities among the inhabitants.

Devanga Weavers of Kuthampully in Kerala

Constituting a quarter of the total looms in India, Tamil Nadu has the highest number of handloom weavers in the country, with both silk and cotton weaving undertaken in a diverse array of techniques.[30] This wide repertoire can be owed to the phenomenon of migration – southward migration of a group of weavers called Saurashtra or Pattunulkaras (from Gujarat) who settled in Madurai in the seventeenth century and developed silk weaving in the state.[31] Generally, most of the weaving communities in South India carry a long history of migration including Kaikkolars, Saliyars, Devangas, Jedras and Saurashtras.[32] At times, permanent weaver migrations of entire families in medieval South India could involve distances of over a thousand kilometres, taking place in parts, over centuries.[33]

Five hundred years ago, upon the request of the King of Kochi, weavers from Mysore in Karnataka moved and settled in a village in Kerala called Kuthampully. Belonging to the Devanga community, the weavers used to create cloth for the King and his family. In the twentieth century, another cross-border migration took place from textile centres in Tamil Nadu to Kuthampully. The proximity between the twin states at the southernmost tip of the country had an immense influence on how weaving developed in Kuthampully, and more broadly in Kerala.

Tamil Nadu hosts some of the largest textile manufacturing industries, both handloom and power loom, specifically centred in Salem, Coimbatore, Erode and Tiruppur. Because weaving, spinning or cotton cultivation, none have a traditional history in Kerala, a lot of cross-pollination takes place from this bordering state in terms of raw materials (yarn and dyes), finished textiles, latest tools and technology and even skilled workers. At present, cotton is procured from Coimbatore, as rolled balls of yarn called *pavu*. The oft-cited cultural difference between the conjoined states is fairly recent. Echoing Rita Kothari's words, "Boundaries do exist; things, spaces and groups do begin and end. But they tend to shade off, merge, graduate".[34] Therefore, any developments on either side of the border cannot be considered in isolation, always exerting mutual influence on one another. In the early 1980s, jacquard was introduced in the village from Tamil Nadu and even today the punch cards are made in and purchased from Coimbatore.[35] The intimacy between the regions is further reflected in the weavers' and traders' familial relations wherein a lot of the daughters of the Devanga community are married off to families in Tiruppur and Coimbatore.[36]

95% of the handlooms in Kuthampully produce weave a pristine, all-white textile with *kasavu* (gold or silver yarn) border. Apart from kasavu border, the *karai* (colour) bordered sari, called Kattikarai, was earlier a regular feature but is now rarely woven in the village and instead sourced from places such as Erode, Salem and Coimbatore in Tamil Nadu.[37] Also, a non-colour pavu is easier to weave as compared to a karai one since it is good for the ageing weaver who possesses a wavering eyesight. The weavers' demographic in Kuthampully is largely defined by this older generation of weavers. Recently, there has been a growing trend in colour screen printing that utilises chemical dyes. Tissue, which has increasingly become a fashionable fabric to be screen-printed upon, is also sourced from Tamil Nadu while the kasavu is sourced from Surat.

At present, handlooms in Kuthampully are getting retrofitted with a motor that speeds up the production process and this has been a growing trend across handloom weaving clusters in India. Another technology intervention has been the double jacquard mechanism which has increasingly gained prominence in Tamil Nadu. Not just raw materials, but migrant weavers from this neighbouring state, who are experts in jacquard weaving in silk, come and weave on the looms of Kuthampully. This 'floating population' of temporary migrant workers live in an impoverished state in small one-room tenements, working collectively in 'weaving sheds'.[38] Away from their families and with easy access to liquor (toddy) in the region, they are often found weaving in an inebriated state. In terms of out-migration, the inhabitants of Kuthampully have not migrated out of the village, not for employment at least. Although children have moved out for marriages and other alliances with Tamil Nadu, as discussed above, which has been a similar case in Kutch, but in sharp contrast to Bengal where a lot of out-migrations have taken place over time.

Notes

1 Murari Jha, Weavers in Early Modern South Asia (Sixteenth–Seventeenth Centuries), In *The Indian Ocean in the Making of Early Modern India*, ed. Pius Malekandathil (UK: Routledge, 2017), 309.
2 Vijaya Ramaswamy, "Alien Weave: Crafts Verses Consumerism," *India International Centre Quarterly* 29, no. 2 (2002): 117–128.
3 Chinmay Tumbe, *India Moving: A History of Migration* (India, Gurugram: Penguin Vintage, 2022).
4 Peter Harnetty, "'Deindustrialization' Revisited: The Handloom Weavers of the Central Provinces of India, c. 1800–1947," *Modern Asian Studies* 25, no. 3 (July 1991): 455–510.
5 Harnetty, "'Deindustrialization' Revisited.".
6 Richard A. Frasca, "Weavers in Pre-Modern South India," *Economic and Political Weekly* (July 1975): 1119–1123.
7 Anjali Karolia, *Traditional Indian Handcrafted Textiles: History, Techniques, Process, Designs Vol II Woven Textiles* (New Delhi: Niyogi Books, 2019), 164.
8 Prasannan Parthasarathi, *The Transition to a Colonial Economy: Weavers, Merchants and Kings in South India, 1720–1800*. No. 7 (Cambridge: Cambridge University Press, 2001), 8.
9 A term I borrow from Rita Kothari, *Memories and Movements: Borders and Communities in Banni Kutch, Gujarat* (New Delhi: Orient BlackSwan, 2013), 29.
10 Tumbe, *India Moving*, 194.
11 For a detailed discussion, see Hameeda Hossain, "The Alienation of Weavers: Impact of the Conflict between the Revenue and Commercial Interests of the East India Company, 1750–1800," The Indian Economic & Social History Review 16, no. 3 (July 1979): 326.
12 As quoted in Hameeda Hossain, "The Alienation of Weavers".
13 Pranav Das, personal communication, July 10, 2023.
14 Niloy Das, personal communication, July 11, 2023.
15 Poulomi Saha, *An Empire of Touch: Women's Political Labor and the Fabrication of East Bengal* (New York: Columbia University Press, 2019), 5.

16 *Bhiga* is an Indian unit to measure land area that can vary between a third of an acre to a complete acre.
17 Pranav Das, personal communication, July 10, 2023.
18 Our Planet II, episode 1, season 2, "Chapter 1: World on the Move," created by Alastair Fothergill, and Keith Scholey, featuring David Attenborough, aired April 5, 2019, on Netflix.
19 Anup Biswas, personal communication, Dhakuria, July 11, 2023.
20 Mekhla chador is a textile traditionally woven in Assam in Northeast India.
21 Biren Kumar Basak, personal communication, July 10, 2023.
22 Kothari, *Memories and Movements*, 2.
23 Kothari, *Memories and Movements*, 5.
24 Archana Shah, *Shifting Sands. Kutch: Textiles, Traditions, Transformations* (Bandhej Books, 2013), 25.
25 Kothari, *Memories and Movements*, 10; Nazanin Hedayat Munroe, *Skilled Immigrants in the Textile and Fashion Industries: Stories from a Globe-Spanning History* (London: Bloomsbury Visual Arts, 2024).
26 Kothari, *Memories and Movements*, 39.
27 P. Sainath, *Everybody Loves a Good Drought: Stories from India's Poorest Districts* (India: Penguin Books India, 1996), 76.
28 Bhamal Jaimalji, personal communication, January 5, 2024.
29 Namori Kaka, personal communication, January 3, 2024.
30 Karolia, *Traditional Indian Handcrafted Textiles*, 227.
31 Karolia, *Traditional Indian Handcrafted Textiles*, 229.
32 Vijaya Ramaswamy, *The Song of the Loom: Weaver Folk Traditions in South India* (India, Kundli: Primus Books, 2013).
33 Tumbe, *India Moving*, 25.
34 Kothari, *Memories and Movements*, 13.
35 Pradeep, personal communication, January 23, 2024.
36 Anandan, personal communication, January 22, 2024.
37 Anandan, personal communication, January 22, 2024.
38 Prabhu, personal communication, January 23, 2024.

Bibliography

Frasca, Richard A. "Weavers in Pre-Modern South India." *Economic and Political Weekly* (July 1975): 1119–1123.

Harnetty, Peter. "'Deindustrialization' Revisited: The Handloom Weavers of the Central Provinces of India, c. 1800–1947." *Modern Asian Studies* 25, no. 3 (July 1991): 455–510.

Hossain, Hameeda. "The Alienation of Weavers: Impact of the Conflict between the Revenue and Commercial Interests of the East India Company, 1750–1800." *The Indian Economic & Social History Review* 16, no. 3 (July 1979): 323–345.

Jha, Murari. "Weavers in Early Modern South Asia (Sixteenth–Seventeenth Centuries)." In *The Indian Ocean in the Making of Early Modern India*, edited by Pius Malekandathil, 291–327. UK: Routledge, 2017.

Karolia, Anjali. *Traditional Indian Handcrafted Textiles: History, Techniques, Process, Designs Vol II Woven Textiles*. New Delhi: Niyogi Books, 2019.

Kothari, Rita. *Memories and Movements: Borders and Communities in Banni Kutch, Gujarat*. New Delhi: Orient BlackSwan, 2013.

Munroe, Nazanin Hedayat. *Skilled Immigrants in the Textile and Fashion Industries: Stories from a Globe-Spanning History*. London: Bloomsbury Visual Arts, 2024.

Parthasarathi, Prasannan. *The Transition to a Colonial Economy: Weavers, Merchants and Kings in South India, 1720–1800*. No. 7. Cambridge: Cambridge University Press, 2001.

Ramaswamy, Vijaya. "Alien Weave: Crafts Verses Consumerism." *India International Centre Quarterly* 29, no. 2 (2002): 117–128.

Ramaswamy, Vijaya. *The Song of the Loom: Weaver Folk Traditions in South India*. India, Kundli: Primus Books, 2013.

Saha, Poulomi. *An Empire of Touch: Women's Political Labor and the Fabrication of East Bengal*. New York: Columbia University Press, 2019.

Shah, Archana. *Shifting Sands. Kutch: Textiles, Traditions, Transformations*. Bandhej Books, 2013.

Sainath, P. *Everybody Loves a Good Drought: Stories from India's Poorest Districts*. India: Penguin Books India, 1996.

Tumbe, Chinmay. *India Moving: A History of Migration*. India, Gurugram: Penguin Vintage, 2022.

4 Women, Weaving and Climate Change

"I feel hot but what to do? Whether it is hot or cold, I have no choice but to work."[1]

Gender forms a key social dimension among the weaving communities in India. For long considered the prerogative of men, women have rarely been designated as the 'weaver', until recently. Women's participation in weaving is largely attributed to their engagement in ancillary activities such as spinning, carding, reeling bobbins, tying weaver's knots, warping and other post-loom processes, at times simultaneities of these tasks make her a more efficient worker. She seamlessly embeds all of these activities within her daily routine while running around chores in the house or undertaking caring responsibilities. A woman's time is thus considered polychronic as opposed to a man's which is largely monochronic, for the most part, engaged in weaving.[2] This gets exacerbated in different regional contexts with a majority of the women in India living straitjacketed lives. This is specifically the case in parts of North and West India where patrilineal families limit her movement within and beyond the threshold of the house.

Considered a normative extension of the hearth, the loom as a non-human entity serves as yet another vertical of her domestic responsibilities. However, because of the scale of the tasks she is engaged in, women's contribution to the handloom industry often goes unnoticed and for the most part, has remained in the shadows – the image of the male weaver being the default imagery one forms in association with the craft. Thus, inadvertently, the history of weaving has largely been the history of men.

Women and Hand Spinning

As a family-run enterprise, weaving is closely tied to the weaver's domestic life with women, children and other members engaged in one or more tasks related to weaving. Yarn spinning was one of the primary activities that was considered a woman's job. In pre-colonial South India, it was undertaken as

DOI: 10.4324/9781003450061-4

a seasonal activity, especially in dry areas, during off-agricultural season.[3] Historian Prasannan Parthasarathi writes in *The Transition to a Colonial Economy*, how spinning acted as a kind of insurance in such terrains and in times of drought, many women would have supported their families through their spinning.[4] So much was the relation between women and spinning that in some parts of the Tamil country, as late as the 1960s, a charkha was included in woman's dowry.[5] A similar narrative from North India discusses how in a pre-partition Punjab, a woman's knowledge of spinning made her marriage-ready.

Despite its strong association with women, spinning has always been undertaken as a part-time occupation by women at home. It was predominantly considered an activity undertaken by widows, maiden mothers, old female *dasis* (women servants), women ascetics and temple female slaves.[6] As is well-known, the English word 'spinster' has origins in the word 'spinning', where a woman has to support herself and thus spins to earn a living.

Spinning was earlier related to the time of the day, for instance, women in Gangetic Bihar used to spin in the afternoons. In fact, the finest cotton yarn was spun by women under thirty who worked early in the morning when the dew was intact on the grass and temperatures were low – the moisture in the air was conducive to the stickiness of the cotton and prevented the threads from breaking.[7] The home-based spinning industry started its slow decline in the early nineteenth century with the invention of spinning jenny in England. Historian Giorgio Riello writes how the spinning machine allowed an eighteenth-century European woman to produce as much yarn as three hundred women in India.[8]

In the present day, mill-spun yarn is used across both handloom and power loom with hand-spun yarn becoming a rarity. Spinning has now been semi-mechanised and mechanised, from charkha to ambar charkha to large-scale spinning in the mills. The decline of both hand spinning and hand weaving was 'almost complete' by 1870.[9] India was now importing instead of exporting, a case in point being the wool that India imports, even though it produces a large quantity annually. In Kutch, where desi oon was once the only wool variety available, Merino is now imported from Australia and New Zealand. The paradoxical presence of an inanimate charkha in Nadia and Kutch is thus denotive of a defunct practice.[10]

Beyond fulfilling their designated tasks, women have also assisted men, especially for a detailed weave such as Jamdani that required the labour of two people to lay the warp, one to weave, two people to render the floral design and another (generally a woman) to tie the threads of the design.[11] Earlier looms had elaborate gears, it took 4–8 days to prepare the warp for a given task and each weaver required at least one woman to help him size the thread and fix it on the loom.[12] At times, the entire process was too tedious and laborious; it is known that communities like Koshtis in South India, used to take several wives to save the cost of hiring workmen.[13]

In keeping with the current trends in sari style, women are found to be engaged in post-loom tasks such as making tassels by twisting and knotting the edges of the sari.[14] Women have also regularly filled in their husbands' seats on the loom, as evidenced in parts of Bengal, where men's out-migration rate is relatively higher. Save for these proxies, the woman as a weaver in its own right is still not a common narrative. *Julaha* or *Bunkar* are words that describe the masculine; there are no feminine terms to describe a woman weaver in any Indian language.

Women Holding the Fort in Nadia

Women as weavers are becoming increasingly visible on the Bengal landscape, although largely filling in men's absences as seen in Nadia. When men out-migrate or shift to an alternative profession, women step in. One of my informants, Pranav Das, says how when the man goes away, the home is empty, leaving women with more time on their hands.[15] Where men have stayed put in the village, women turn to weaving to supplement their husband's income. With rising inflation, sole reliance on a single family member's income usually does not suffice, so women have to take up additional work which substantially increases their workload. Dohra Ahmad writes in the introduction to her anthology that those who stay home, whether by choice or otherwise also belong in the complex story of migration.[16] And so were the women in Nadia.

Surprisingly, it was only recently that women took to weaving in large numbers in Phulia. Under a Central Government scheme, a series of workshops were organised in 2016 that compelled more people to weave.[17] One of the most influential master craftsmen-turned-businesspersons and a jamdani weaver-designer in the region, Biren Kumar Basak engages over 2000 women weavers across multiple villages. Biren elaborates how the woman would multitask, toggling between the kitchen and loom, several times a day.[18]

A total of 50 women from Phulia and nearby villages learnt to weave. The wage was a huge incentive for people to join the training, however, there was differential pay for men and women. While women used to get paid 300 INR, men received 700–800 INR per sari. Women can weave three saris a week which generates an income of 1500 INR per week. Women are now using the skills learnt during the workshops, to weave and support their husbands in running the household. The training has given women *himmat* (strength) and confidence to weave as a means of earning.[19]

The differential pay factor is a recurring issue in Bengal. In Raghavpur, near Habibpur, women do not get paid a lot, as one of the weavers Purnima

Sarkar discusses. She says that she has no choice but to sell through a mahajan because she has no money to buy her own warp.[20] In a day, she spends a total of 7–10 hours weaving. She wraps up all her chores for the day, right in the morning and sits down to weave until 10 in the night. Women are also found to be weaving in more congested spaces as compared to men. Weaver Konika Das (aged 25) works in a room for one, a mere 5 by 5 feet, with the loom in the front and the small kitchen facing her back.[21] She takes roughly 2–3 days to weave because she has small kids to tend to. She thinks if she drops all work for the day and works on the loom at a stretch, she can finish the sari in a day. She gets paid 100 INR for a plain sari and 120 INR if some motifs are rendered on the body.

For Archana Rajvanshi, a 47-year-old weaver in Udaypur village, weaving is not a craft, but a means to an end.[22] As a widow, she learnt the skill from her father and was enterprising enough to employ three women. They collectively work in a small area adjacent to her house. An erstwhile spinner, it has been ten years since Archana deserted the charkha, its dormant existence gracing the courtyard of her house, symbolic of an era passed. Till 1965, hand spinning could be seen in Bengal but now the yarn is directly sourced from the mills. Spinning can be found in other districts across Bengal such as Murshidabad, but this too is not spinning by hand but a semi-mechanised process carried out on an ambar charkha.[23] The spinning equipment resembling a charkha that women use to reel bobbins in Bengal can often be mistaken for a spinning wheel.

The situation, however, in the villages of Santipur appears more bleak than in Phulia. A women's group in Baigachi in Santipur, where three young women were found working within a small, congested settlement, unlike saris that women usually weave, they were weaving *odhnas* (dupattas) that women do not even wear in the village. The weaving sound was faster here, it could be because they were working with a coarser yarn, creating a looser weave as compared to other weaving establishments in the village. Particularly with women weavers, there is a sharp contrast in what the weaver is making versus what she is wearing. Where male weavers sit bare-chested with a checked lungi as a bottom, women are often seen wearing cheap imitations of a handloom sari, commonly a mill-made one in polyester or mixed fibre. Being inexpensive and coupled with the ease of draping and maintenance have led to their increased popularity in the village environment.

The Women Warpers of Kutch

In the arid landscape of Bhujodi, wearing what one would call a half-sari, a woman can be found holding a wand-like stick in one hand, transferring the yarn right to left and left to right on vertical pegs nailed on a large wooden frame.[24] At first glance, it might seem she is working magic into thin air with the stick, but upon careful observation, the fine yarn comes into view. Called *taana*, what she is essentially doing is creating the warp from the yarn reeled on bobbins before it is sized and eventually laid on the loom. Women have been engaging in this activity for decades, whenever they find time in between household activities.

As one would naturally think, there is no drum warping (warping undertaken on a circular frame) operational in Kutch. This is mainly because all tools and equipment in the region are centred around the weaving of desi oon. The warp length is usually smaller, 25–30 metres from which 8–10 shawls can be woven. This length is too small to work with on the drum where a minimum of 200 metres is required. So, ladies at home fix *khillis* (small rods) in the wall and create the warp. The wooden structure thus created is called a spool rack or warping creel with the entire process termed sectional peg warping (Figure 4.1).[25]

Additionally, women can also be found working on mirror embroidery on the body of the sari and braiding tassels along the edge of the sari defining the pallu.[26] Women are also involved in the making of *kanji*, a starch used in the sizing process, prepared by boiling wheat flour for a long duration.[27] Other supporting tasks were discovered too where women could be found engaged. For instance, weaver Govind Naran's daughter in Bhujodi used to work on a cotton farm, five kilometres away. Called 'Kapas Kheti', she used to travel quite a stretch to pluck cotton.[28] Ladies are also considered the fixers of things – their role as menders reflects their larger role in salvaging things and taking responsibility for a crisis, small or big. Thus, women are regularly relied upon for tasks such as fixing yarn hanks and in the post-dyeing stage, fixing any colour difference.

On asking a bobbin winder, Deval Behan (aged 52), in Varnora village, if she has felt any change in the climate; she replied with a negation. When I asked her if it had become hotter, she gave an acerbic response, "*Mahsoos toh hota hai par kya karein*" (I feel hot but what to do? Whether it is hot or cold, I have no choice but to work). Starting her day at 7 am, Deval Behan winds bobbins for 6–8 hours a day, working till noon and then again from 2–5 pm. She does not sleep during the day and instead gets an early sleep in the night. Her husband, Bhamal Jaimalji explains how women's work is more in weaving-related activities. "Men only have to weave, women do a lot of things on the other hand," as one of my respondents Hamirji remarked.[29] He added how women's involvement in weaving-related activities is significantly larger, around 60% while men's is only 40%.

Figure 4.1 A woman undertaking peg warping in Bhujodi, Kutch.

Women Weavers in Kuthampully

As oral sources revealed, hand-spinning has never been undertaken in the village of Kuthampully in Kerala. Yarns were always sourced from the bordering state of Tamil Nadu, from regions such as Coimbatore or Salem, that are notorious not only for their polluting factories but also for the pernicious working conditions of workers in the textile industries.[30]

Women also play an active role in street warping where members from the neighbourhood gather each morning (around 7–10 people) to help roll the weaver's *pavu* on the beam that will then be fitted on the loom to start the weaving process. The act of rolling does not take so much time as does disentangling the yarn and removing any joints. The women insert themselves in the web and deftly pull out the intertwined threads and re-join each one of them. This task of separating the threads demands dexterity (Figure 4.2). Another crucial skill that women are engaged in is the tying of the weaver's knot. When the entire warp has been woven the fabric is cut and to attach a new set of warp threads on the loom, each thread is

Figure 4.2 Street warping in process in the streets of Kuthampully, Kerala.

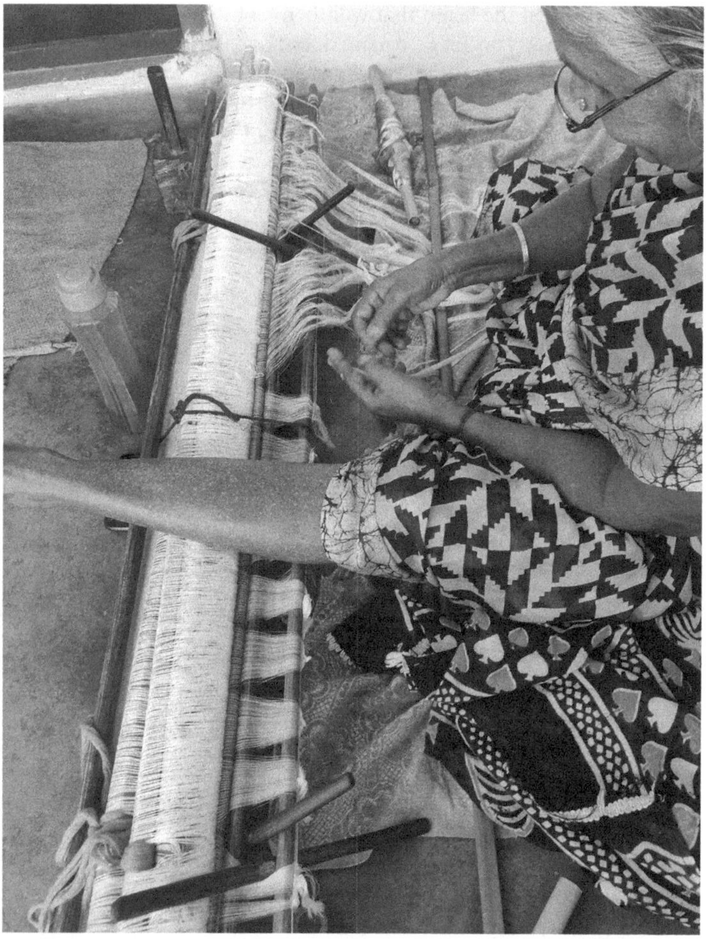

Figure 4.3 A woman tying weaver's knots in Kuthampully Kerala.

reattached one by one to the corresponding threads on the beam. There are around 2200 such yarns in the warp that need individual tying (Figure 4.3). The tying of a weaver's knot requires a high level of precision and deftness of fingers and remains the domain of women in Kuthampully.

Notes

1 Deval Behan, personal communication, January 5, 2024.
2 Edward T. Hall, *The Hidden Dimension* (New York: Anchor Books, 1982), 173.

3 Prasannan Parthasarathi, *The Transition to a Colonial Economy: Weavers, Merchants and Kings in South India, 1720–1800*. No. 7 (Cambridge: Cambridge University Press, 2001), 58.
4 Parthasarathi, *Transition to Colonial Economy*, 58.
5 Parthasarathi, *Transition to Colonial Economy*, 58–59.
6 Kiran Singh, *Textiles in Ancient India*, 100–101.
7 See Eric Broudy, *The Book of Looms: A History of the Handloom from Ancient Times to the Present* (UK, Hanover: University Press of New England, 1993), 54, 276; Romesh Chunder Dutt, *The Economic History of India: Under Early British Rule, 1757–1837*. Vol. 1. (Publications Division, Ministry of Information and Broadcasting, Government of India, 1960), 232–235.
8 Giorgio Riello, *Cotton: The Fabric that Made the Modern World* (New York: Cambridge University Press, 2013), xxiv.
9 David Clingingsmith and Jeffrey G. Williamson, "Mughal Decline, Climate Change, and Britain's Industrial Ascent: An Integrated Perspective on India's 18th and 19th Century Deindustrialization," (November 2005), 17.
10 There was found no trace of even a physical structure of a charkha in Kuthampully.
11 As quoted in Hameeda Hossain, "The Alienation of Weavers: Impact of the Conflict between the Revenue and Commercial Interests of the East India Company, 1750–1800," *The Indian Economic & Social History Review* 16, no. 3 (July 1979): 323–345.
12 Peter Harnetty, "'Deindustrialization' Revisited: The Handloom Weavers of the Central Provinces of India, c. 1800–1947," *Modern Asian Studies* 25, no. 3 (July 1991): 455–510.
13 Harnetty, "'Deindustrialization' Revisited", 458.
14 This was observed both in Kutch and Phulia.
15 Pranav Das, personal communication, July 12, 2023.
16 Dohra Ahmad, *The Penguin Book of Migration Literature Departures Arrivals Generations Returns* (New York: Penguin Books, 2019), xxiv.
17 Pranav Das, personal communication, July 12, 2023.
18 Biren Kumar Basak, personal communication, July 10, 2023.
19 Pranav Das, personal communication, July 12, 2023.
20 Purnima Sarkar, personal communication, July 12, 2023.
21 Anonymous weaver, personal communication, July 14, 2023.
22 Archana Rajvanshi, personal communication, July 13, 2023.
23 Archana Shah, *Crafting a Future: Stories of Indian Textiles and Sustainable Practices* (New Delhi: Niyogi Books, 2021), 83.
24 A half-sari is constituted by draping the *odhani* over a *ghagra*, paired with a backless *choli* top.
25 Anjali Karolia, *Traditional Indian Handcrafted Textiles: History, Techniques, Process, Designs Vol II Woven Textiles* (New Delhi: Niyogi Books, 2019), 23.
26 These are just for the sari and weave, there are multiple embroidery styles and other crafts in the textile-rich region of Kutch.
27 Bhamal Jaimalji, personal communication, January 5, 2024.
28 Govind Naran, personal communication, January 1, 2024.

29 Hamirji Vishram, personal communication, January 2, 2024.

30 Indumathy, "A Study on Quality of Work Life Among Workers with Special Reference to Textile Industry in Tirupur District-A Textile Hub," *Journal of Contemporary Management Research* 6, no. 1 (March 2012): 78; K. Logasakthi and K. Rajagopal, "A Study on Employee Health, Safety and Welfare Measures of Chemical Industry in the View of Salem Region," *International Journal of Research in Business Management* 1, no. 1 (June 2013): 1–10; A. Valarmathi and Hema Bhalakarishnan, "A Study on Quality of Work Life in Textile Sector in and Around Coimbatore District," *Journal of Business Management & Social Sciences Research (JBM&SSR)* 2, no. 2 (February 2013): 42–46.

Bibliography

Ahmad, Dohra. *The Penguin Book of Migration Literature Departures Arrivals Generations Returns*. New York: Penguin Books, 2019.

Broudy, Eric. *The Book of Looms: A History of the Handloom from Ancient Times to the Present*. UK, Hanover: University Press of New England, 1993.

Clingingsmith, David and Jeffrey G. Williamson. "Mughal Decline, Climate Change, and Britain's Industrial Ascent: An Integrated Perspective on India's 18th and 19th Century Deindustrialization." (November 2005).

Dutt, Romesh Chunder. *The Economic History of India: Under Early British Rule, 1757–1837*. Vol. 1. Publications Division, Ministry of Information and Broadcasting, Government of India, 1960.

Frater, Judy. "Warp and Weft: Tradition and Change, Craftsmen and Innovation in Bhujodi." *Marg* 73, no. 4 (2022): 130–135.

Hall, Edward T. *The Hidden Dimension*. New York: Anchor Books, 1982.

Harnetty, Peter. "'Deindustrialization' Revisited: The Handloom Weavers of the Central Provinces of India, c. 1800–1947." *Modern Asian Studies* 25, no. 3 (July 1991): 455–510.

Hossain, Hameeda. "The Alienation of Weavers: Impact of the Conflict between the Revenue and Commercial Interests of the East India Company, 1750–1800." *The Indian Economic & Social History Review* 16, no. 3 (July 1979): 323–345.

Indumathy, R. "A Study on Quality of Work Life Among Workers with Special Reference to Textile Industry in Tirupur District-A Textile Hub." *Journal of Contemporary Management Research* 6, no. 1 (March 2012): 78.

Karolia, Anjali. *Traditional Indian Handcrafted Textiles: History, Techniques, Process, Designs Vol II Woven Textiles*. New Delhi: Niyogi Books, 2019.

Logasakthi, K. and K. Rajagopal. "A Study on Employee Health, Safety and Welfare Measures of Chemical Industry in the View of Salem Region." *International Journal of Research in Business Management* 1, no. 1 (June 2013): 1–10.

Parthasarathi, Prasannan. *The Transition to a Colonial Economy: Weavers, Merchants and Kings in South India, 1720–1800*. No. 7. Cambridge: Cambridge University Press, 2001.

Riello, Giorgio. *Cotton: The Fabric that Made the Modern World*. New York: Cambridge University Press, 2013.

Shah, Archana. *Crafting a Future: Stories of Indian Textiles and Sustainable Practices*. New Delhi: Niyogi Books, 2021.

Singh, Kiran. *Textiles in Ancient India*. India, Varanasi: Vishwavidyalaya Prakashan, 1994.

Valarmathi, A. and Hema Bhalakarishnan. "A Study on Quality of Work Life in Textile Sector in and Around Coimbatore District." *Journal of Business Management & Social Sciences Research (JBM&SSR)* 2, no. 2 (February 2013): 42–46.

5 Loom(ing) Hierarchies in Nadia

> "*Jo tanti hai na, wo tanti hee rehta hai.*" (A weaver stays a weaver forever)[1]

> "In future, if someone has to see handwoven fabric, they will have to go to the museum – that's the future of handloom, just like how we see muslin in the museum today."[2]

It is paradoxical that the everyday weaver in India is poor and the makers of the finest cloth in Bengal (muslin and jamdani) are even poorer. The weavers who have always been marvelled at for the dexterity and nimbleness of their, fingers that weaver is poor. As opposed to how they are positioned today, weaving and spinning were venerable occupations in the ancient Rig Vedic society. The status of a weaver on the lower rungs of society in the present day is rather an anomaly. Weavers are craftspersons in their own right, however, they and their labour have often been marginalised.

Tucked right above the largest delta in the world, the Nadia district in the state of West Bengal has been an ancient site of handloom weaving for over 500 years, so much so that the textile craft of jamdani is proverbial to Bengal. Referred to as figured muslin, the region created this evanescent-like textile that was considered one of the finest to have ever been conceived by human hands. For centuries, this textile garnered huge connoisseurship and patronage, particularly during the Mughal reign in India. While aristocracy used to wear the fine muslin in Bengal, including jamdani, the common man was draped in *tants* or plain cotton fabric. It was woven in the old village of Santipur in Nadia, a prominent site of muslin production in Bengal until the early eighteenth century. Facing tough competition from the English cotton industry and the subsequent surge in imports of imitated muslin, the mill-made cloth from Manchester precipitated the decline of this industry in Santipur. This change was irreversible and the Bengal handloom sector has never been able to regain its allure.

DOI: 10.4324/9781003450061-5

Phooti Kapas that once was

Not just the virtuosity of the indigent weaver but the secret of the fine quality of muslin resided in a special variety of cotton called Phooti Kapas that used to grow in an area of deltaic Bengal, now geographically located in present-day Bangladesh. One of my interviewees, Niloy Das traced his fingers on a printed map of the Sundarbans, showing the stretch of 40 kilometres where phooti kapas once used to grow. He stressed the importance of this fecund zone, how the alluvial soil, the climate of the Gangetic plain and its proximity to a river, collectively created favourable conditions for the cultivation of this cotton variety.

In the early to mid-nineteenth century, the Bengal landscape in East India was redesigned by colonial administrators, with the rivers controlled. This led to the loss of the phooti kapas cotton variety.[3] This compromised the 'climatological and cultural' dimensions of the landscape which was necessary in the crafting of this textile.[4] The weavers and farmers were thus forced to cultivate indigo and opium. Phooti kapas was dependent not just on the fluctuations in seasonal monsoon but also on factors including the proximity to the sea and the temperature change between warmer river water and colder seawater, all bearing the brunt of climate change in the early twentieth century.[5] There is no denying the fact that Bengal's climatic conditions were once deemed to be ideal for cotton growing and weaving.

There are five rivers crisscrossing through the district of Nadia – Bhagirathi, Churni, Mathabhanga, Ichamati and Jalangi.[6] This proximity to a water body helped in connecting and establishing erstwhile trade networks with other parts of the subcontinent as well as exporting to regions of what constitutes present-day Afghanistan, Iran, Greece and Turkey.[7]

Today, the original muslin is no longer woven in the subcontinent. Both the climate and soil were cardinal elements for the sustenance of phooti kapas, now neither that weather is there, nor the muslin exists.[8] The alluvial soil of West Bengal in India is not good for cotton growing and as of now, no cotton grows in Bengal.[9] Weaving clusters in both East and West India wholly rely on South India for cotton, procured from states such as Maharashtra and Tamil Nadu. Even yarn in Bangladesh is sourced from these Indian states. The loss of a cotton variety was also the loss of indigenous tools. For instance, the kapas used to be cleaned and carded with the jawbone of *baolee* fish, a local in Bengal.[10]

Present-Day Weaving in Bengal

The weaver caste in Bengal comprises *tantis*, *kalibartas*, *bagdis* and *jugis* with *tanti* becoming a colloquial word for a weaver in the region. Traditionally, weavers belong to the Basak community, particularly concentrated in the Phulia village. Nearly 3,50,000 households are involved in handloom weaving in the state, in rural areas across four districts of Nadia, Hooghly, Bardhaman and Bankura.[11] The geographical focus of this chapter is a new settlement called Phulia in the Nadia district. Within Nadia, various weaving clusters are known for different sari weaving styles and different loom setups: Santipur for Santipuri sari and Phulia for Tangail and Jamdani sari. The names become remnants of lands the textiles originally travel from. While Phulia is characterised by the transparency of its gossamer-like weave, the characteristic of a Santipuri sari is its elaborate border detail. Weaving in the Nadai district is as old as the 1400s and specifically in Santipur, weaving can be traced back about 500 years.[12] The intermingling and positioning of the diversity of weaving techniques within Bengal has led to hybrid forms emerging with the various names used interchangeably today.

Unlike other weaving techniques, jamdani is not a single weaver's job and often requires the combined skill of two or more weavers to create the figurative design. Jamdani is characteristically known for both the manually undertaken extra weft technique as well as the infallibility of the weaver's fingers. A technique worked on the reverse, this 'silent dialogue' between the weaver's eye and his hand is what lends the textile an ethereal quality.[13] In tandem with recent trends of thinner borders, minimum motifs and less elaborate designs rendered in a looser weave, the weaver takes a minimum of one and a maximum of two days to finish a sari if the warp is ready and set on the loom and no breakage happens while weaving. Contrarily, a sari on a power loom takes a minimum of two hours which makes a day's output of roughly 4–5 saris.

Constituted of 300 small villages, there are roughly 70,000 weavers in and around Phulia.[14] Over the past few decades, looms in Phulia have plummeted in their numbers.[15] With different occupational preferences, the younger generation from the Basak community does not wish to become weavers because they could see their own doom.[16] This form of upward mobility of weavers although it ameliorates their families' economic conditions, it also leads to deskilling of the weavers. The children now want to conduct business instead of weaving, the latter deemed to be a time-intensive occupation with low returns.[17]

The Indispensable Mahajan

The weaving landscape of Nadia, and Bengal largely, is ruled by the Mahajans – traditional moneylenders who have existed in the system for centuries now. The economy of Phulia is maintained by them, creating hierarchies that reveal hidden inequalities. Essentially like middlemen, mahajans facilitate the distribution of raw materials including yarn and loom to the weavers who would not be able to afford these themselves while also facilitating market access for them by selling their products. Through their wielded power, the mahajans dictate the weaving sector in a way that the weaver cannot operate in isolation from the mahajans and thus is hugely dependent on them for his sustenance. Although the collaboration between the two has not always been fair, weavers in Phulia revere mahajans as Gods since they were the ones who offered weavers (let it be any work) during the 2020 pandemic. The mahajans in Bengal have thus earned the sobriquet of *maalik*, the master or God.

This system of middlemen has existed since the late seventeenth and eighteenth centuries when Bengal emerged as an important textile market for Europe.[18] As part of the controlled economy, the mahajans provided the raw materials to the weaver and in some cases, loans as well. The government provides looms to mahajans, who then roll these out to individual weavers.[19] Mahajans procure yarn from the market as cones which are then distributed across allied workers who undertake the dyeing, drumming and beaming, with the weaver receiving the ready warp rolled over onto the beam.[20] In Phulia, weavers sell locally, mostly to master weaver-turned-entrepreneurs such as Biren Kumar Basak or other master weavers. They will have to source warp directly if they wish to sell the woven textiles on their own.

In his research on the silk handloom industry of Nadia, Chandan Roy discusses three categories of weavers – entrepreneur weavers, labourer weavers and cooperative fold weavers.[21] Weavers who could invest money have transitioned into master weavers, employing individual weavers as wage labourers, who get paid at piece rates, as little as 200 INR for a sari.[22] Many master weavers have now become mahajans. "They have big mansions and have now set up a couple of machines," as one of my informants says, with some mahajans these days standing for the elections as well, so much appears to have shifted.[23]

Biren Kumar Basak is the most popular weaver-seller in the district. Biren is a Padma Shri awardee, renowned worldwide for his narrative jamdanis. He has been weaving for the last 60 years; he learnt to weave when he was just ten. Biren's fame reaches far and wide – his brand's hoardings can be spotted all over Nadia, from a campaign affixed onto a small shop at the Santipur station platform to bigger billboards along the highway. His house in Chatkatala village mirrors this popularity with a bungalow-like mansion where he both resides and conducts business. But Biren is a parvenu, his wealth is new. In the 1960s, his family migrated from Tangail district in present-day Bangladesh to Phulia in India. His father used to conduct door-to-door *feri* (peddling), an old way of selling saris by weavers. Today, Biren churns out a weekly production of 5,000–8,000 metres of handloom. He is mainly known for his Dhakai Jamdani and Meenakari saris that retail for as high as five lakh Indian rupees.

In terms of direct market access, there are weekly haats in Santipur where weavers get to sell directly. 95% of the saris sold here are products of power loom although sellers use the façade of 'pure handloom' ever so often.[24] In the entire market spread over three floors, one may discover a handloom or two only upon a very careful observation.

The Sonic Environment of Nadia

Located along the river Hooghly (also known as Bhagirathi), the landscape of Phulia is dotted with nondescript tin sheds, each akin to a mini freight container, under which sweat-glazed bodies of the weaver toil on the loom. The shiny, reflecting appearance of the tin features oddly in the bucolic setting with plasterless, exposed-brick houses conveying the thrifty nature of the village. The placement of sheds is representative of the informal organisation of weaving communities in Phulia.

The crafting of a landscape or the choice of building material, as archaeologist makes note of in his book *Craeft*, is reflective of the social and economic history of the people and the lands they come from.[25] These tin homes had a marked presence in undivided Bengal as well. With recurring floods and villages constantly inundated, at times for months at a stretch, the tin house as a construction technique was the easiest to build and rebuild from limited and easily accessible resources and so the migrants carried this material aesthetic too with them, along with their skill of weaving.

Upon entering Phulia, one is left disenchanted with a bedlam of multiple sounds, of the juddering tenor of power looms interspersed with the dulcet rhythm of handloom, at times both thriving under the same roof – this dissonance between the two is stark and obvious. Between the staccato of handloom and the falsetto of power loom, the sounds of nature appear lost. At times this gets punctuated with Manna Dey's song in Bangla thrown into the sound mix. The even pace of the power loom thus stands in a stark monotony to the unevenness and cadences of the handloom.

It is startling how weavers have got accustomed to these sounds that make up their everyday. How does it feel to live in an environment brimming with deafening weaving noise? A similar sentiment is evoked in Kazuya Minoura's article that discusses how the residents of Fujiyoshida, a power loom centre in Japan, consider this noise as the 'sound of work' which then becomes a way for them to get attuned to the machine's working – it is their livelihood after all.[26] Minoura writes, "When an industry is deeply connected with a community, the sounds can be taken as an acceptable and even appropriate element of the [sic] area".[27] I wonder if this is the case with Phulia as well, the sound morphing into a 'lullaby' as Minoura comments. Like a factory running from home, these vibrations and reverberations deeply influence the everyday lives of weavers and their families and other inhabitants of the village but because it supports their living it does not seem to bother them much.

Tin Sheds and Trapped Heat

In the metal enclosure of tin homes, it was evident that a lot of heat would be trapped and reproduced throughout the day. Research suggests that the combination of humidity and polluted air is lethal.[28] Although there is no direct connection between working under tin sheds and the act of weaving itself, however, in a region where the humidity levels are ever on the rise, it has proved uncomfortably helpful to work in the searing heat. Although the weaver is at unease, he has to bear with it because the *maad* (starch paste) that the weaver regularly rubs on the warp has to dry up fast for a distinct glaze. If the maad-glazed warp does not receive the required heat, the textile-in-making will remain wet, thereby increasing the possibility of a black spot surfacing on the fabric. If several power looms are in operation within a small space, it generates a cumulative effect with increased heat in the air. The situation gets worse, particularly in workspaces where handloom and power loom share the same space.

As compared to Phulia, Santipur is differently spatialised. With denser weaver settlements and serried houses, the Muslim quarters appear more marginalised than their Hindu counterparts within Santipur and this is also the case in Phulia. The workspaces are more congested with over a hundred different weaving communities working in Santipur.[29] The sound of every handloom across Nadia is not the same. With scarcely any handlooms to be found, the sonic environment of Santipur is dominated by an even greater number of power looms than in Phulia, barring a handful.

The fast, even-paced mechanical sounds emanating from the power loom are indicative of a rapid shift in the last century with the introduction of the jacquard mechanism in the 1930s. From an erstwhile painstaking technique of manual extra weft, the cutwork technique has become a faster way to produce the textile; the sleight of the jamdani weaver's fingers gets discounted in the process. Before 2010, there were no power looms in Phulia and with the newer Rapier looms interpolated in the last few years, per day production has risen to 30 pieces where a power loom was earlier churning 5–7 pieces a day.[30]

Traditional Tools and Methods

Where earlier, there were all pit looms in Phulia, these have now been replaced with frame looms. Few weavers still continue to weave on pit looms because they cannot afford to purchase new looms. As a tokenistic support to the handloom sector of Bengal, the State Government started providing frame looms to weavers across various clusters, however, hardly any weavers ended up using it. When asked why, Pranav, an erstwhile weaver's son, provided an interesting analogy – "When a person who eats by hand is given a fork and a knife to eat, will they be able to have food with them? They simply cannot!" The looms given by the government suffered a similar fate. Made of cheap-quality wood (unlike Sal that good looms are made of), and without any accompanying materials, the loom requires further adjustments before the weaver can work on it.[31] So instead of spending time and money in setting the loom right, weavers desert it altogether.

When the weather is dry, during the day, weavers put a pot of water under the warp which helps keep the yarn moist. Upon being asked if this is still the practice, one of my interviewees said, "Those days are gone, neither that muslin remains nor that technique."[32] However, during monsoon, when it gets very wet and the maad-applied yarn dries more slowly than usual, a bed of burning wooden shavings is kept under the warp which aids in faster drying of the threads.[33]

Effects of the Changing Climate

There is no gainsaying the fact that the industrialisation of the handloom sector has altered weaving patterns, however, the changing climate has played an important part too. The increased heat is creating problems although most of the weavers are unable to draw connections of this warming to climate change. Niloy Das shares how, at times, when it gets very hot, the tin sheds break down too.[34]

These days, weavers have side fans or tiny fans whirring on top of their heads, affixed on their looms to cope with peak summer heat. During *sookha garmi* (dry summer), when there is no water vapour in the air, it gets even more difficult to weave in the afternoons. Because both the warp and the weft are sized with precision, it becomes hard to maintain their strength. Due to an apparent lack of moisture, the yarn becomes stiffer which increases its chances of breakage. This subsequently demands an increased effort on the weaver's part in manually joining the broken threads. The more dry the weather gets, the more challenging it becomes for the weaver. If the threads are not sized altogether, this issue of stiffness and breakage may no longer be there but leaving the warp unstarched will affect the quality of the resultant textile while also considering that this practice of starching is in tandem with the Bengali style of draping the paper-thin, crisp sari.[35]

The yarn is also more prone to breaking when the humidity is less. In contrast, when humidity is higher, the yarn becomes loose, reducing its chances of breaking. Especially viscose, a man-made fibre that is now increasingly used for borders in the sari is the most difficult to weave in moisture-laden weather owing to its elasticity. With increased moisture, elasticity increases too, making it difficult to maintain the proportions of the warp and the weft while weaving.[36] It is important to note here that because a lot of traditional processes have either been mechanised or outsourced, the impact of the changing climate is felt less. For instance, earlier, the yarn dyeing process was cumbrous, labour-intensive and time-consuming and any change in rainfall patterns would significantly impact this process. But now with the ready availability of ready-made, powdered colour, the disruptions in the weather no longer hold the earlier grave consequences.

Another effect of the changing climate is less production since more weaving is now undertaken in the morning hours and less in the evening. Biren Kumar Basak mentions how an over-reliance on machines is making the weavers lethargic where they were much more hardworking before.[37] A mere one-tenth of the weavers wake up at 4 am and begin their day to weave.

Floods are a rare occurrence in the Nadia district except for once when all looms had to be lifted. While I was conducting fieldwork in Phulia and Santipur, it rained erratically. Biren mentions how the weavers are used to the heavy rains as a way of life and thus are ever-prepared to cope with any extremities.[38] During rains, the warp threads become more taut than usual; the lengthening and contraction of the yarns become a concern.

When it rains, because a pit loom is under the ground level, *maati* (soil) gets damp, and if the soil touches the warp, the textile will develop a stain on the yarn. This spot is nearly impossible to remove owing to a particular gas in the soil, as Biren Kumar Basak revealed.[39] Both high and low humidity are problematic for weaving. In wet weather, high moisture results in a variation in threads since it alters their density and strength. One of my interviewees, Niloy, asks me, "Hand weaving is completely dependent on the climate. Have you ever seen weaving happening in a place that is exposed to dry weather"? I replied with the example of Kutch and he responded rhetorically, "What kind of material is it? – It is thick material and people in Kutch have adapted to their climate". In *sookha* (dry) areas, a different technique is adopted for weaving. In Purulia, a dry plateau region in West Bengal, one cannot weave cotton and instead, tussar is woven because the weather is suitable for the rearing of silkworms.[40]

Effects are also noticeable on the weavers' bodies. If it is very hot, as a human it is extremely difficult to work, as Rekha Biswas, a woman weaver in Panpara village lamented.[41] Particularly if the weaver is a heart patient, it takes extra effort to weave because of the increased pressure exerted with handloom weaving that gets aggravated when it is hotter. The work becomes strenuous, requiring a lot of effort and labour on part of the weaver. Deepak, an old weaver in Basakpara village in Phulia, wove an intricate jamdani with floral detail on the *pallu* and this section itself took him fifteen days and in total, the sari took him three months to complete. He says it takes him longer to weave because, in hot weather, the production slows down since it is difficult to sit in one place for longer hours.[42] "*Kasht hota hai shareer ko*" (The body goes through a painful experience), as another woman weaver, Archana Rajvanshi exclaims.[43] In winter, however, weaving is better. Monsoon is just fine, but summer is difficult in comparison. So weavers weave in the wee hours during the summer months.

Conclusion

While working on a green temple border sari, Hazari Sheikh, a 58-year-old weaver in Santipur, gets paid a mere sum of 150 INR for a sari which takes him six hours to weave. Contrarily, on a power loom, ten saris can be generated in that much time.[44] Skilled weavers in villages in the Nadia district still live a penurious existence. There was one household in Babla village near Santipur that had three members sharing one loom. The weaver is finding it difficult to arrange a minimum of two meals a day through his practice of weaving. Unable to generate enough income to feed themselves, they choose to continue because they do not know any other work apart from weaving.

"If the weaver gets at least 500–700 INR a day, then only he can run a family, otherwise how will he run a family?", Biren expresses. With such living extremities, Niloy is right when he says, "Who would want to weave?". As one of my interviewees commented, "*tanti ki ladki ka shaadi nahi hota*" (it is difficult to get a weaver's daughter married today unless she belongs to a wealthy family). That is the extent to which the status of the craft has shifted.

In the last two decades, the power looms have encroached upon the handlooms across villages in Phulia. There are no statistics on the actual ratio of power loom to handloom, but as per a guesstimate, 80% of the looms today in Nadia are power looms.[45] To buy a power loom, a weaver needs an investment of a minimum of half a lakh that can extend to over a lakh sometimes which is a substantial amount for the handloom weaver. Rapier looms that increase the production eightfold, come at a staggering price of over fifteen lakhs. However, a sari churned by a Rapier can cost as little as 200 INR; these looms have thus intensified the already competitive market. It is an indisputable fact that what power loom did to handloom, now Rapier is doing to power loom. Where weavers earlier were deserting handlooms for power looms, now they are deserting their power looms for Rapier looms.

The village landscape in Phulia today alternates with curiously padlocked tin sheds, a moment frozen in time. A corollary of the pandemic-induced lockdown in early 2020, where temporary weavers went back home, deserting their looms in abeyance, not knowing if they would return. With many villages depopulated, the lockdown became a key event for the weavers so much so that it has become a reference point for many weavers while explaining events in chronic time.

The changing climate has also exacerbated the deeply entrenched inequalities where Phulia is already walled in by both the disingenuousness of mahajans and the tough competition from power looms. There are other issues too that these weaving settlements face including regular interruptions in the electrical power supply. Even when the supply goes off for just 15–20 minutes, with no arrangements for power backup, the weavers' workflow gets significantly disrupted.

A repeated sentiment bemoaned by weavers was how one day this will all be gone.[46] There are government bodies responsible for overseeing the various handloom clusters in India, but the state of the weavers remains dismal. Facing ever-increasing competition from the industrial sector and alternative labour markets, a stronger support and market for handloom is the only way to sustain both the skill and the craft.

Notes

1 Pranav Das, personal communication, July 10, 2023.
2 Niloy Das, personal communication, July 11, 2023. Niloy is a migration researcher undertaking a study on weaving communities and records changes in weaving communities post 1947 migration.
3 Labib Hossain, "A Critical Reading of the Dry and Permanent Ground through the Practice of Muslin Weaving," *Monsoon [+ other] Grounds. University of Westminster London* (2020): 113–120.
4 Hossain, "A Critical Reading," 117.
5 M. Saiful Islam, *Muslin! Our Story* (Drik Picture Library, 2016).
6 Chandan Roy, "The Silk Handloom Industry in Nadia District of West Bengal: A Study on its History, Performance & Current Problems," *New Man International Journal of Multidisciplinary Studies* 4, no. 7 (July 2017): 50–66.
7 Roy, "The Silk Handloom Industry," 51–53.
8 Niloy Das, personal communication, July 11, 2023.
9 Since black soil is a necessary criterion for growing cotton.
10 Anjali Karolia, Traditional Indian Handcrafted Textiles: History, Techniques, Process, Designs Vol II Woven Textiles (New Delhi: Niyogi Books, 2019), 140.
11 Karolia, *Traditional Indian Handcrafted*, 137.
12 Roy, "The Silk Handloom Industry," 53.
13 An expression I borrow from Victoria Mitchell, "Drawing Threads from Sight to Site," *Textile* 4, no. 3 (2006): 340–361.
14 Archana Shah, *Crafting a Future: Stories of Indian Textiles and Sustainable Practices* (New Delhi: Niyogi Books, 2021).

15 Phulia had 75,000 looms in early 2,000, the number fell to 35,000 in 2010 and eventually to 20,000 in 2017. See Roy, "The Silk Handloom Industry," 55.
16 Pranav Das, personal communication, July 10, 2023.
17 Biren Kumar Basak, personal communication, July 10, 2023.
18 However, mahajans are not middlemen per se. Also see Murari Jha, "Weavers in Early Modern South Asia (Sixteenth–Seventeenth Centuries)," In *The Indian Ocean in the Making of Early Modern India*, edited by Pius Malekandathil, 291–383 (UK: Routledge, 2017), 301.
19 Samir Das, personal communication, July 12, 2023.
20 The drumming system makes warping significantly easier.
21 Roy, "The Silk Handloom Industry," 61.
22 Niloy Das, personal communication, July 11, 2023.
23 Pranav Das, personal communication, July 10, 2023.
24 I reckon the percentage is even higher.
25 Alexander Langlands, *Craeft: An Enquiry into the Origins and True Meaning of Traditional Crafts* (New York: Norton, 2018), 169.
26 Kazuya Minoura, "Life with Weaving Noise in Fujiyoshida: A Soundscape as a Commons," In *Proc. 14th Global Conference of the International Association for the Study of the Commons*, 3–7. 2013.
27 Minoura, "Life with Weaving Noise," 1.
28 C. Lubelska, Utilizing Oral History in the Study of Textile History, In *Disentangling Textiles: Techniques for the Study of Designed* Objects, edited by Mary Schoeser and Christine Boydell, 167–175 (London: Middlesex University Press, 1999), 169.
29 Ashis Mitra, Prabir Kumar Choudhuri and Arup Mukherjee, "A Diagnostic Report on Cluster Development Programme of Santipur Handloom Cluster, Nadia, West Bengal Part I–Evolution of the Cluster and Cluster Analysis," (2009).
30 Niloy Das, personal communication, July 11, 2023; Biren Kumar Basak, personal communication, July 10, 2023.
31 A sturdy and resilient wood, sal stays intact for 20–30 years, is not prone to any termites or insects and unaffected by monsoons.
32 Niloy Das, personal communication, July 11, 2023
33 Pranav Das, personal communication, July 10, 2023.
34 Niloy Das, personal communication, July 11, 2023.
35 I thank Niloy Das for these insights, personal communication, July 11, 2023.
36 Niloy Das, personal communication, July 11, 2023.
37 Biren Kumar Basak, personal communication, July 10, 2023.
38 Biren Kumar Basak, personal communication, July 10, 2023.
39 Biren Kumar Basak, personal communication, July 10, 2023.
40 Niloy Das, personal communication, July 11, 2023.
41 Rekha Biswas, personal communication, July 13, 2023.
42 Deepak, personal communication, July 13, 2023.
43 Archana Rajvanshi, personal communication, July 13, 2023.

44 Hazari Sheikh, personal communication, July 10, 2023.
45 Niloy Das's assumption, personal communication, July 11, 2023.
46 Pranav Das, personal communication, July 10, 2023.

Bibliography

Hossain, Labib. "A Critical Reading of the Dry and Permanent Ground through the Practice of Muslin Weaving." *Monsoon [+ other] Grounds. University of Westminster London* (2020): 113–120.

Islam, M. Saiful. *Muslin! Our Story*. Drik Picture Library, 2016.

Jha, Murari. "Weavers in Early Modern South Asia (Sixteenth–Seventeenth Centuries)." In *The Indian Ocean in the Making of Early Modern India*, edited by Pius Malekandathil, 291–327. UK: Routledge, 2017.

Karolia, Anjali. *Traditional Indian Handcrafted Textiles: History, Techniques, Process, Designs Vol II Woven Textiles*. New Delhi: Niyogi Books, 2019.

Langlands, Alexander. *Craeft: An Enquiry into the Origins and True Meaning of Traditional Crafts*. New York: Norton, 2018.

Lubleska, C. "Utilizing Oral History in the Study of Textile History." In *Disentangling Textiles: Techniques for the Study of Designed Objects*, edited by Mary Schoeser and Christine Boydell, 167–175. London: Middlesex University Press, 1999.

Minoura, Kazuya. "Life with Weaving Noise in Fujiyoshida: A Soundscape as a Commons." In *Proc. 14th Global Conference of the International Association for the Study of the Commons*, 3–7. 2013.

Mitchell, Victoria. "Drawing Threads from Sight to Site." *Textile* 4, no. 3 (2006): 340–361.

Mitra, Ashis, Prabir Kumar Choudhuri and Arup Mukherjee. "A Diagnostic Report on Cluster Development Programme of Shantipur Handloom Cluster, Nadia, West Bengal Part I–Evolution of the cluster and cluster analysis." (2009).

Roy, Chandan. "The Silk Handloom Industry in Nadia District of West Bengal: A Study on its History, Performance & Current Problems." *New Man International Journal of Multidisciplinary Studies* 4, no. 7 (July 2017): 50–66.

Shah, Archana. *Crafting a Future: Stories of Indian Textiles and Sustainable Practices*. New Delhi: Niyogi Books, 2021.

6 Weaving Indigenous Wisdom in Kutch

> "If it is land, you can sell it. But if it is Earth, can you sell it? So now you have to decide if it is land or Earth".[1]

> "I do not need money; if I get a good night's sleep, that is more than enough".[2]

"Kutch bohot sookha pradesh hai" (Kutch is a very dry province), rued Premji Velji Siju, one of my interviewees.[3] Tucked in a corner on the westernmost tip of the country, India's largest district stretches across a wide portion of the dry land in Gujarat. The nearest city of Bhuj sits ten kilometres away. The region witnesses extremely low temperatures in the morning and evening and extremely high temperatures in the afternoon. The entire Bhuj-Kutch area speaks the Kutchi language although the official language across workplaces in Bhuj and around is Hindi or Gujarati.[4] Not just its remoteness, the sparsely populated Kutch stands out anachronistically in the geography of the state it is officially a part of. In fact, the name Kutch is older than Gujarat itself.[5] Being a British Protectorate and governed by rulers, the artisans do not feel associated with Gujarat owing to the region's differently evolved culture, habits, customs and language. Both their distinct identity and the geography where they are positioned have resulted in the preservation of their rich miscellany of crafts that Kutch today is renowned the world over. Every village in the region is traditionally known for its distinguished craft practice – from embroidery and weaving to leather work and woodwork.

Kutch was an erstwhile site of the Indus Valley civilisation; the ancient city of Dholavira is located just 130 kilometres off Bhuj. A series of climatic and seismic changes altered the landscape, making it uninhabitable.[6] Archana Shah eloquently describes the modern undulating landscape of Kutch in her book *Shifting Sands*, defining the region as:

> "from the salt plains of the Great Rann and the Little Rann to the grasslands of Banni, the Charri-Dhand wetlands and marshes around

DOI: 10.4324/9781003450061-6

the Black Hills, the plains of Lakhpat and Jakhau, the mangrove swamps of Mundra and Koteshwar, and the Gulf of Kutch with its coral reefs and creeks."[7]

Many of these topological features have slowly vanished from the view. One such village is Bhujodi, where the Vankar weaving community engages in handloom weaving of woollen blankets and shawls and more recently the Bhujodi sari and other dress materials. The eponym 'Vankar', an inflexion of the word 'bunkar', translates as a weaver in English. Vankar is thus a referent to their occupation. Not just Bhujodi, but weaving is also undertaken in other villages in Kutch namely Sarli, Varnora, Kotai, Dhokda, Jamthada, Ramper Vekra, Adhoi, Kotaya, Awadhnagar, Ganakorda and Mathala.[8] In Bhujodi, at present, there are 250 homes out of which 150 are weaver homes with at least one weaver per family.

Weather-Dependent Processes

The raw materials for most of the pre-loom and post-loom activities were earlier sourced directly from the forests, which the inhabitants refer to as *jadi-buti* (herbs). One such type was *Vrat* or *Pankada*, a rain-fed wild onion. Following a cumbersome process that entailed boiling the vegetable and grinding it to a paste, vrat was used to starch the indigenous variety of wool called 'desi oon'.[9] Starching as a process, follows warping and is done right before the warp is ready to be set on the loom. An essential process especially for natural fibres, starching stiffens the fibres so that it is easier to weave on the loom as well as avoid any yarn breakage.[10] Vrat can no longer be found in the forests of Kutch and has been replaced with *kanji*, a paste created from *atta* (whole wheat flour or bajra flour) following a process of boiling, soaking and drying.

A total of 25–30 metres in length, the warp, called *taar* in Kutch, is starched taut in an open area, the entire process termed *paed.*[11] The worker meticulously applies kanji on the warp, using a large comb called *kaangad* – an indigenous brush crafted from local wild grass.[12] Interestingly, weavers in Kutch refer to the starching process as painting! Particularly during summer months, the weavers have to work faster because as the *kanji* dries, the threads stick to each other whereby each thread has to be individually separated.

A young man, Prakash, is found starching dyed kala cotton on a winter morning nearing noon (figure 6.1). When asked how much time it usually takes to finish the process, he replies, "*Mausam ke hisaab se*!" (Depending on the weather). He adds, "It is windy today so it will take 1.5–2 hours to finish. If threads break in between, then maybe an hour more." They can perform the process in the evenings as well, although there is no fixed time as such, relying solely on the worker's intuition about the weather. In winter, although paed can be done at any time of the day, *kadak* (harsh) heat is not good as the taar dries up fast and they will have to simultaneously single out the threads, performing two parallel processes at the same time. Prakash cannot start very early in the morning either because it will take a lot of time to dry then; the yarn needs a little bit of warmth in the weather too.

Figure 6.1 Street sizing in process in Bhujodi, Kutch.

Perceiving the Changing Climate

There was a certain similitude in the responses evoked when weavers were asked if there have been noticeable changes in the climate and how these have influenced the practice of weaving. The answers were similar in that they could not articulate the changes, even though they felt the climate changing tremendously in their lifetime.

Rains in Kutch have never been continuous and have always followed an erratic nature. But for the last decade or two, monsoon has been perceived to be regular, raining 2–4 times a year, over 1–2 months, which is deemed good by the weavers because it cools the weather a bit.[13] Otherwise, as Vankar Poonam Arjan lamented, it was all "*akaal akaal akaal dushkaar*" (drought, drought, drought – misery), with a severe drought in 1968, followed by a famine in 1987. The *nami* (moisture) in the air has increased as well over the years. More nami makes it difficult for the weaver to separate the threads while increasing the chances of its breaking. Frequent rains in the region have also enabled farming of grains such as moong, jowar, guar, bajra, wheat as well as *kapas*. Kapas grows in plenitude now in Kutch, although this cotton is not to be confused with kala cotton. The former is the Bt type, while the latter is an indigenous rain-fed variety that only grows in the desert terrains of Gujarat such as Wagad and Limbdi near Surendranagar in Saurashtra district.[14]

During the monsoon season, looms are kept completely shut. "If 80% of work is happening right now, only 20% of work happens during rains", says weaver Siddharth Mangariya.[15] The scant rain is not enough to create problems for weavers such as the filling of pit looms, but there are other issues that it carries. The main reason to suspend weaving during a rainy spell is that black spots appear on the surface of the fabric on the loom if rainwater falls, owing to its reaction with the fibre.[16] The reed, an important part of the loom and wrought from bamboo, swells up too when it rains.

Gopal Vankar, the sole yarn seller in Bhujodi asks rhetorically, "*Thandi kahan hai? Pehle thandi zyada thi, ab nahi hai*" (Where is the cold? Earlier it used to be very cold, now it is not). During the peak winter month of January, people used to sit in front of the fire, even during afternoons. I travelled in January and the way we were sitting in the sun, earlier one could not think of sitting outside like this in winter. The erstwhile cooler climate would allow weavers to weave for six months at a stretch, the winter is not the same anymore.

The weaving months were also linked to their festival calendar. Vankar Shamji Vishram discusses how earlier the calendar was 'perfect'– between Diwali and Holi (two main Hindu festivals), there used to be constant work, but those six months have shrunk in comparison to the present day. Now, during summer, work can happen only after 4 pm. Additionally, electricity is an essential requirement where earlier even fans were not needed. As another weaver, Namori Kaka, revealed, "*Garmi kabhi mehsoos hee nahi hui*" (I never felt hot only).[17] In fact, till the 1970s there were hardly any fans in the region. Even at present, only a few families in Bhujodi have Air Conditioners (ACs).

Climate Changes, Culture Changes, Yarn Changes

In Kutch, the yarn is treated with reverence. Rabaris have always believed that wool is a sacred yarn with unique qualities. It keeps them cool in summer and warm in winter owing to its insulating properties that help maintain the right body temperature.[18] Because the winter season is no longer cold enough in Kutch today, warm clothing sells less. Earlier, ahead of the winter season, all wool products were kept ready which is not the case anymore. Now only when an order is placed that the product is woven on the loom. As a result, many shawl-weaving setups have shut down owing to no demand; the demand is climate-dependent in this case. Additionally, the ways that a shawl was draped earlier have altered as well. "No one carries a shawl anymore", says Gopal Vankar; the older way is no longer considered 'trendy'. Another respondent, Siddharth Mangariya, adds, "Who wants to wear a shawl when there is a sweater and a jacket? So, we had to modernise the shawl. We created a jacket or a poncho-like garment out of the shawl."[19] Even though demand for shawls has seen a dip, the number of weavers in Bhujodi has increased, the market for winter blankets and shawls being substituted with those of sari and dress material.

For every weaver, how they perceive the changing weather varies. According to one of my interviewees, Namori Kaka, who was relatively well aware of the changing climate, not just in Bhujodi but surrounding villages as well, the shift in seasons is the main effect of climate change.[20] Another weaver in Varnora, Poonam Arjan notes how earlier winters were short, lasting only a month but in their short duration, they would cast a severely dry spell. Winters were painful; people would suffer from body pains and flayed skin. Now, no matter how long winters continue, it is still considered not that dry, which Poonam Arjan regards as good weather. "The heat is the main problem", adds Poonam. He explains that it gets so hot during peak summer months that they are unable to work during the day, so they have to get up early to weave.

Both a weaver and a yarn seller, Gopal Vankar opened the first yarn shop in Bhujodi in mid-2023. Where earlier weavers had to take a trip all the way to Bhuj to source the yarn, his enterprise fills a much-need gap, as looms in the village are on the rise. He says that the fine yarn (called Super), is fetched from Ludhiana in Punjab. He discussed how although Kutch is known for its sheep and goat herders, wool is not that readily accessible in the region, the reason being the absence of any spinning facility – there is no one to spin the sheared wool. The fibre is sent to Ludhiana to be spun and is eventually processed there. As per his knowledge, no spinning has taken place in Kutch in the last thirty years. He feels the reason is that nobody wants to undertake slow, hard work with everybody being in a rush so much so that a weaver wants to start and finish a sari in a day, which is possible to do now.

Although there are no power looms in the entire Kutch region, the yarn used in handloom is the same as used in power looms elsewhere in the country. A region that traditionally used only pit looms, it was only in the aftermath of the cataclysmic earthquake of 2001, that destroyed 70% of the weaver households in Bhujodi, that frame looms were introduced to the village.[21]

Climate's Favourite Crop: Kala Cotton

Indigenous to the Little Rann of Kutch, Kala Cotton is one of the oldest varieties of cotton in the world. A short staple, the life of kala cotton is purely dependent on the rain. The large-scale weaving of kala cotton is, however, a new phenomenon in Kutch. The traditional looms in Kutch were made for weaving desi oon to make the khadi attire of Ahir men.[22] Kala cotton is not to be confused with *kapas*, however, which is used to denote the Bt variety of cotton that was introduced to the region in the 1950s.[23] It was followed by softer merino in the 1960s and Super wool from Ludhiana in the 1980s.

Fly-shuttle was introduced in the region because of an increase in the use of merino.[24] Earlier, throw shuttle looms were used to weave a blanket or *odhani* but after 1950, the *phatka* (shot) loom, also known as semi-mechanised loom was introduced.[25] Later, the region was acquainted with acrylic, which was deemed easier to handle on the loom where desi oon is known to be the most difficult to work with. Tussar silk came in much later, introduced to the desert looms in 2007. Lastly, fine mill-made cotton (also called fine cotton) has only entered the market in recent years and is sourced from Ahmedabad in Gujarat.[26]

Weaving with kala cotton requires *chhaun* (shade), so excessive sunlight at times can pose a problem. This is the reason why the looms are always located in a slightly covered area, at inside-outside junctures, the threshold of spaces. It is rarely kept inside a closed room, except in the present times. Namori Kaka discussed how when it gets hotter, the warp becomes hard and stiff. It does not remain as soft which is the hallmark quality of kala cotton.[27] Kala cotton is purchased from the market as a cone with refined quality so while earlier it was difficult to get used to working with it on the loom, this is not the case anymore. In contrast, the mill-made yarn that comes with a finer count takes much longer to weave with.

The changing climate has impacted this rain-fed crop too. The supply of kala cotton has decreased over time due to irregular rainfall or shifts in the monsoon season. Where once desi oon dominated the weaving landscape, new materials have shared, and even surpassed that space in the last few decades. Desi oon is barely considered useful now for the 3–4 months that define the winter season in Kutch and not for the remainder of summer.[28] With an extended summer season, the weaving of kala cotton has been on the rise, constituting 80% of handwoven textiles produced in Bhujodi today. An all-season fabric, kala cotton is cool in summer and warm in winter. In addition, since it is made in natural ways, it is good for the skin too.

Spinning with Desi Oon

The spinning of desi oon is indigenous to the Kutch region. From 1984 to 2000, desi oon was all handspun but towards the end of the twentieth century, the practice ceased and was deemed nearly extinct. In later years, with newer initiatives and younger people becoming involved, desi oon is undergoing a revival. Since 2016, Khamir, a body that works with preserving crafts and the cultural ecology of Kutch, has been working with desi oon. Ranaji, an important member of this project from its very beginning, mentions how he procures wool from local pastoralists while discussing changes he has witnessed in the last fifteen years.[29] Ranaji mentions how each year, he collects three tonnes of wool from communities such as Maldharis, Rabaris, Rajputs and a few other herders as well. When he began, Ranaji was involved in training women across eighteen villages – some who already knew the skill and others who were new learners. In all, 350 women are engaged in hand spinning across the villages of Varnora, Kukma, Gharoli, Bhadroi, Kukadsar, Yashoda Dham, Ajapar, Modasa, Lodai, Ratnal, Makhiana and Mindiyala, out of which, Ranaji works with 150 women on a regular basis.

Typically, Maldharis, after shearing their animals' wool, would discard it in the jungle, since in the absence of any spinner, the raw material was rendered useless. Maldharis are known to keep five types of sheep – Dumi, Patanwadi, Desang, Kaari and Marwari. Dumi wool is the one that falls off naturally from the animals. Ranaji procures all kinds from the Maldharis, barring the Marwari, because the wool is much thicker, especially when compared to Patanwadi wool which is softer and has a longer staple. He sources this wool from Samosra village and Lakhpat Taluka in Kutch.

Previously, wool was procured from Kutch and Rajasthan. However, with a decrease in the number of *pashupaalaks* (animal keepers) today, the fibre is sheared only twice a year, and the resulting fibre is of a shorter staple which does not produce a uniform yarn. Naranbhai Siju, who runs a weaver enterprise called Kutchi carpets, is one of the few carpet weavers in Bhujodi.[30] While the warp he uses is entirely cotton-based, the weft is a blend of wool and jute. Earlier, he used to buy wool from a retailer, the prices were erratic and the quality was loose and poor which made it difficult to weave. Now he sources wool from Bikaner, a large supply of which lasts him a year. Bikaner mandi, considered one of the largest wool markets in the country, has around 150–200 such factories that process wool. Wool from Bikaner gets exported to other Indian cities as well, such as Badoli (Uttar Pradesh) and Panipat (Haryana) which have large carpet industries. With the third largest sheep population globally, India produces around 45 kilograms of wool every year but a majority of it is discarded because of its short staple and coarse texture.[31] Earlier, the wool in Bikaner used to come from within the state but now gets imported from countries such as China, UAE, Sri Lanka, Australia and New Zealand.

Although revival projects in hand spinning such as Khamir's are active, the resulting price of the wool is much higher, nearing 1000 INR per kg which raises the price of the woven textile. Naranbhai sources from Bikaner machine-spun yarn at 200 INR per kg. Another weaver, Bhamal Jaimalji in Varnora, discusses how earlier no weaver would make yarn at home, it was solely the job of Rabaris or Maldharis. "A weaver does not make yarn; a weaver's role was only to weave and never to spin because if the weaver starts spinning, what will the spinners do?"[32] His father used to say that if weavers started spinning, they would be eating away the spinner's subsistence. Spinning was also age-related – women would usually spin after the age of forty and embroider in their younger years.

An unstitched piece of textile in desi oon that Rabari women wear over their heads and bodies, *Ludi* is still produced in Kutch, but it costs a lot more since rarely anyone spins the yarn now. Earlier Rabari women used to spin their own wool and then hand it over to the weavers to weave a ludi for them. Now since the wool is sourced from places in Rajasthan such as Barmer, Bikaner and Jodhpur, it becomes expensive which has advanced the weavers' labour wages while subsequently increasing the price of the ludi. An original ludi can now cost somewhere between 3000 and 5000 INR which is expensive for villagers, who cannot afford to wear such a costly garment on a daily basis.[33]

Maintaining Reciprocal Relationships

In a riverless land, animal husbandry forms the main source of livelihood. Others include agriculture (with the little arable land that the desert can afford), mining and the newly constructed industries. Rabaris, traditionally a herding community, originally kept camels but now the earlier categorisation for various pastoralists remains no longer fixed.[34] Women belonging to this community would spin yarn from the wool they sheared from the goats and sheep they raised. To clarify, Rabaris do not practice weaving. As the pasture area shrunk, the number of pastoralists decreased substantially over the years. The government leased away their land to multiple industries across the Kutch region. Left with no land to graze their animals on, the ecological balance was disturbed. Master weaver Shamji Vishram from Bhujodi explains that the animals need *kudrat ki hawa* and *kudrat ka khana* (natural air and natural food) to give good produce.[35] Also, young Rabari men are no longer stepping into the fields and have instead adopted alternative professions, preferring to drive trucks or rickshaws.

Craftwork in Kutch was traditionally community-based, with the various communities interconnected. For instance, Meghwals and Rabaris lived a symbiotic existence – wherever Rabaris stayed, Meghwals used to stay adjacent to them.[36] This was because Meghwals practised weaving (hence called Vankars) and would weave textiles for the Rabari womenfolk. For this, the latter would provide their animals' wool. The Rabaris would provide thread, and Vankars would weave. In this traditional form of customisation, weavers crafted ludi, *pachhedi* (skirt cloth for women), *dhabla* (blanket) and *khathi* (shoulder cloth) – elements of the traditional attire of Rabari women.

Ranaji explains how in 1982, he would get paid a small sum of 15 INR for weaving a ludi. He was asked what he needed in return, which could be bajra, jaggery, milk or ghee. Earlier, *haath* (hand) was used as a unit of length instead of a metre.[37] A woman's shawl measures 10 haath while a man's is 20 haath. This double-length worked perfectly well for the peripatetic herder who used to wear a single layer during the day and double it up in the night, while he sleeps. It also acted as a protection from unpredictable rains. Similarly, weight was measured not in grams but in mugs. The cost of the ludi that Ranaji made was calculated in mugs too and one or two mugs of food items were generally given in exchange for a ludi.

This barter economy which enabled a strong partnership, has roots in the age-old jajmani system that entailed the traditional exchange of labour and services for grain and fodder.[38] But after the partition of 1947, the new cotton textile industry of the 50s shifted the dynamic. This *kutir* (cottage) as Naranbhai Siju mentioned, soon became a business.[39] However, some Rabaris still come and buy *odhani* in pure wool from the Vankars. Even though it is rendered expensive, traditional exchanges continue to be maintained.[40] Ranaji says when any of his sisters have a wedding in the village, he makes a ludi for her, it is just that she should give him six months' notice.

Deemed 'untouchables', Meghwals were earlier proscribed from freely mixing with the Rabaris. Where the relations were earlier characterised by acts of sullying, now Meghwals and Rabaris thrive together even though it is widely discussed how caste consciousness is greater today than in the 1950s.[41] In the context of the original wearers, when Kutchi weave is compared to other textiles, master weaver Shamji Vishram has an interesting analysis to provide. The primal wearers of Kutchi weave were the Rabaris, Maldharis and Barwars. He discusses the example of fine muslin jamdani, considered a textile of the plutocrat and whose original wearers were always the richest customers or the royal family. The market for both jamdani and Kutchi weave was different and strongly dependent on the associations of class. The *butis* (motifs) on Kutchi weave, where the extra weft yarn moves from left to right, gets tightly interlocked before it moves the other way. This is in contrast to the extra weft technique in jamdani where the yarn moves smoothly from left to right and the reverse without any locking at the corners. The recognition jamdani received was owing to its wearers which accorded a higher value to the textile. Going by that account, a weaver in Bengal should get paid more than a weaver in Kutch, which is however not the case, as discussed in the previous chapter.

The reason for the success of the handloom sector in Kutch can be attributed to the *kutumbh parivar* (joint family) and collaboration among people at multiple levels. "*Akele ka kaam nahi hai, pariwar bhot zaruri hai*" (This is not the work of a single person, the family is an intrinsic element), says weaver Hamirji Vishram. He says of his younger brother, Shamji Vishram, how he is considered the most innovative out of all the five brothers. He travels worldwide and has received immense exposure.[42] But his success is backed up by his four brothers. While all of them practised weaving earlier, they are now engaged in one or the other aspects of their thriving business. One brother oversees the weaving workshop, another does indigo dyeing, and another handles the accounts.

"Weavers never thought that the people who work for us are our workers, they are like an extended family", says Shamji. This communitarian philosophy and kinship is still what Kutch is rooted in. I am reminded of Robin Wall Kimmerer's words here when she writes, "Cultures of gratitude must also be cultures of reciprocity. Each person, human or not, is bound to every other in a reciprocal relationship."[43] But after the earthquake of 2001 in Bhuj, weavers feel that this philosophy has shifted, transitioning to "*Akela khao, akela piyo*" (Eat alone, drink alone).[44] Many relationships have been reconfigured such as those between shearers and herders. Earlier, members of the Lavas community would travel from Barmer to Kutch for shearing purposes, who would be provided with some wool in exchange.[45] Now they no longer make this long journey to shear the wool.

Wisdom, Spirituality and Interconnectedness

A textile wholesaler in Bhujodi, Siddharth Mangariya's workspace was much cooler owing to the concrete floor of his studio. Alexander Langlands discussed in his book how the immediate environment is a determinant of crafts and the raw materials used.[46] Siddharth went on to describe three types of looms considered indigenous to Kutch. The first is called Motlasar which is completely hand-operated with no *fatka* (shuttle) attachment and the pit is dug out in the open. This forms one of the most inchoate and rudimentary structures for a loom. The second type is called Khadasar, a pit loom where one can weave slightly faster than a Motlasar. The third type is called Lakdasar or Khodasar, a frame loom that is raised from the ground and can be placed anywhere in the absence of a pit. *Khoda* in English translates to a horse, and the loom is called such because it can be moved and stationed anywhere. This kind of loom is, however, more prone to shaking and vibration unlike the first two where the loom is fixed and there is limited movement.[47] Frame looms were introduced in the region after the earthquake.[48] Siddharth himself was found working on a pit loom that is 40–50 years old which his grandfather used to work on as well.

Kutch was also known for its repertoire of indigenous dyeing techniques; weavers once used to possess a rich knowledge of dyes. One such indigenous method was shared by weaver Poonam Arjan who described how a pale pink colour is extracted from the cochineal insect, that often feeds on the growing kapas. After the medicine is sprayed on the kapas, any insects on the leaves fall off, which are then collected and crushed and dye is extracted from them.[49] While indigo dyeing is a continuing practice, other dye colours come in ready-made powder form ready to be mixed in water.

Archana Shah writes in the preface to her book *Shifting Sands*, "At a time when the world is looking urgently at conserving the precious resources of the planet, the traditional wisdom of the people of Kutch certainly offers many lessons that we simply cannot allow to fade into oblivion."[50] In a region where scarcity is the norm, craftspeople have developed a certain habitus based on their lived experiences. Indians are renowned for their use of intuition over intellect, an intuition considered more developed and evolved than others.[51] The Kutch region stands for multiple skills coupled with the prescience of weavers, creating these sets of 'inferential knowledge', a kind of knowledge that is based on experience.

Umaid Shree Bhai is a first-generation weaver in Bhujodi who works as a job worker, and mentioned how his father was a labourer. When Umaid moved from Bhachau to Bhujodi, he learnt to weave and has been weaving for the last 15 years. "I don't need money; if I get a good night's sleep, that's more than enough", he says.[52] The lives of the inhabitants of the region are centred around tradition, myths and stories which go on to define their worldview. Focusing on this interface between weavers, oral traditions, and folklore that Vijaya Ramaswamy calls a 'complex weave', the next few sections are a retelling of these very stories and belief systems.[53] A reflection of the weavers' slower pace of working, my conversations with them were expectedly replete with long interludes.

Case Study 1: Vankar Shamji Vishram

A master weaver, Shamji Vishram emerged as an artisan-entrepreneur at the turn of this century, amassing several accolades, so much so that his name is now synonymous with weaving in Bhujodi. His knowledge of handlooms is evident in the way he can guess which part of India a textile has been woven simply by looking at the marks the beating would have generated along the sides of the textile. A great raconteur, for Shamji, everything is interlinked and interconnected. My conversation with him was full of quips, he was ever ready with rejoinders. He was neatly organising his inventory when we turned up unannounced, only to leave after three long hours.

"*Mausam badla, paani badla*" (When the weather changed, the water changed too). He referred to climate change as *hawa badlav* (a change in the air) while forming the water cycle flow with his cupped hands. As he had heard his elders say, the climate changes all the time but he felt an acute change in the last 20–25 years, a change equivalent to what happens in half a decade. He feels the underlying cause is the social and economic change that has transpired over the years. And this has become so big that all the other cycles – water pollution, change in air quality, changes in villages and changes at home are linked to this larger shift.

A change in climate is also felt by the inhabitants with the setting up of industries and their subsequent effect on water bodies. Shamji expresses his views, "I don't see this as development, that you do everything as you wish. That is not development". This rhetoric of development surfaced multiple times in my conversation with him. He adds,

> "We all might live separately but we all are tied together. In the new development, no one is tied to one another, so everyone makes the other person responsible. Because of that, no one wants to take

> any responsibility and until we do that, this will keep on continuing as is."

He shares how in 1970, pure groundwater used to come to about fifteen feet. His elders had a well at the back of the house and one would drink directly from it. Seeing everyone drinking water from the plastic bottles now, he says

> "I do not see this as development, I cannot. Even if you have money, if you do not eat the right food, why are you living? One does not live for money… Everything is mine, yet nothing is mine. The change in climate is also because we are living just for ourselves – *Khud ke liye jeena*. The more we live for ourselves, the change in climate is inevitable because one ends up thinking about others."

He believes that cultural shifts have happened because of this, "We think, I need everything. Whatever I sow, I want more rewards, even if the other person gets affected, I do not care. Greed has become everything". He adds,

> "If you add salt in measured amounts in food, then only it is edible, right? If you add more salt, what will happen? That is how I was taught [through metaphors]. I do not know how children are taught in the city."

With a worldview that was unlike a city dweller's, he elaborates on the balanced rural ecology that once prevailed,

> "When a new village is set up, it is named just like how a child is named. So when 835 years ago, Bhujodi was set up, it was given a name – *Rabarivaas* (Residence of Rabaris). At that time, only Rabaris were there. They had sheep, goats, camels and cows in large numbers; they had everything. Whatever these sheep and goats ate, their *gobar* (cow dung) inadvertently contained a new seed. So, if she eats a peanut, her dung will also contain one and where she drops that dung, a peanut sapling will grow at that spot. Wherever *pashupaalaks* go, they always give something to the *kudrat* (nature); they are givers. Earlier the land was vacant for them, they had good earnings and good food and they used to support the kudrat. Other people used to derive food from that land. So if we talk about the ecological balance, no one used to disturb the other person."

Shamji perceived nature as an equal participant in this inherent circular economy model. He went on to explain how earlier the year was neatly segregated into quarters based on the four seasons.

> "Three months a year, our elders used to farm the land. Whatever they would harvest, it would last them an entire year. For another three months, they would weave. For another three, they would do leather work in their spare time – make *jutis* and chappals and for the remaining three months, they would do nothing and instead travel and meet their relatives. If a relative in some other village needs people to work on his land, we would travel and help that person and come back and when it would be our time, they would come over. So three months would go away like this. We do not go on any vacation. In the night, the entire family comes together and chats for a couple of hours, ruminating on why we have come here [on Earth]. How you happened to be here, it was something that was decided long back that today you would be here, visiting me. All these things are not taught these days. Because of all these changes, everything else is changing, that's what I feel."

Earlier, and still in some parts of India, farming and weaving were co-constitutive in generational livelihoods – the weavers' lifestyle used to be balanced and season-dependent. Shamji had a very positive outlook on life. He says,

> "I deny that I am doing business. I always say that I am doing it for fun because business cannot be done by me. The day I think of what I do as a business, it will become a burden and I do not want to walk with any burden. I want to work but I also want to be happy."

The Many Entanglements Between Body, Cloth and Poetry

In my discussions with Siddharth Mangariya, a weaver in Bhujodi, he spoke about the embodied labour of the weaver while labouring on the loom. How the weaver works with his entire body found resonance in Norris' writing where she discusses how "Every inch of cloth can reveal the weaver's mood, especially when they are tired, distracted or careless with the beating."[54] This 'attentive material engagement' in the weaver's encounters with the loom involves the "skilled positioning of the whole body through posturing, gesturing, active touch or anticipatory sensing."[55] Although weaving and this 'bodily-kinaesthetic intelligence', as artist Bruce Metcalf frames it, are inextricably connected, there is much more that lends the craft its unique nature.[56]

The Vankars of Bhujodi can be heard humming songs while performing weaving; I could not help but be drawn towards these whispers. This comes as no surprise since this is the case with other weaving communities in India as well and has been of much interest to scholars.[57] Revered as carriers of culture, songs constitute one of the many living traditions of Kutch.

A master weaver, Naranbhia Siju shares why weavers sing these songs.

> "Earlier people used to herd their animals, go to the jungle or collect honey, lac or gum, do farming or engage in construction work, for instance, digging grounds. So after doing an entire day's hard work, when they would come back in the night, whom do they share their pains with? It was the God. There used to be no concept of a temple or an idol, they would light a diya sometimes but that was it. God existed only in their minds and hearts, a feeling they termed as Swami (or Dhani baba in Gujarati). They would pick up their material, stone or wood and create music with it which became a means to share their heart with the God and that is how the bhajan *parampara* (tradition) started."

In the absence of any form of entertainment earlier, bhajans became one of the mediums by which the weaver would entertain himself and those around him. To support their singing, weavers play a range of musical instruments, from harmonium, table and dholak to contemporary ones such as violin and guitar. Many of these instruments are crafted by the weaver himself, from scratch. For instance, weaver Bhamal Jaimalji's *iktara* (a single-stringed musical instrument) was created from a dried vegetable *tandu* (pumpkin), the handle was made from bamboo and the front was finished with goatskin. Now these songs and instruments have become a part of their custom.

Songs thus served as a medium for the weavers' *abhivyakti* (expressions) and what came out of their hearts was termed *ardaas* (prayer). Historically, many craftspeople in ancient India have been recorded as expressing their feelings in the form of bhajans. Some sants would weave, some would engage in leatherwork, and they made work their devotion – their way of worship. As an everyday ritual, before sitting on the loom, a weaver would chant a *shlok* which has, however, somewhat drifted away in present times.[58]

Premji Velji Siju, an octogenarian, who has long left the loom owing to his ageing body, is considered the keystone in the bhajans sung in Bhujodi and around. He narrates how some 300–400 years ago, an old *bunkar* started this singing ritual, that is now called *kabirvaani*. Kabir was a weaver-poet from the old city of Kashi (now Benaras), a place renowned for its brocade weaves the world over. Born in a family of Muslim weavers, Kabir's poems, as Purushottam Agrawal discusses are characterised by "the constant interaction and dialogue between the 'inside' and the 'outside'."[59] This inner and outer space that his poems speak of resonates with the weavers lives and work. While working on the loom, the singing of bhajans limn the world of the weavers. The bhajans are not mere recitations of Kabir's but the weavers have adapted these songs to their language, creating an entirely new vocabulary of expression.

The weavers while sitting on the loom creates a notional world for himself that helps build concentration – it needs focus to work on the filament-like yarn. Namori Kaka, a weaver in Bhujodi, spoke of twenty principles of living a life on which Kabir's songs were based. In present times, however, these precepts have tapered off to a mere five. Nevertheless, Kabir's songs are imbued with spiritual notes which speak to "*Jeevan kaise jeena hai*" (How to live one's life?). How to enjoy the world? How to fulfil one's responsibilities? How to give to society? How not to be jealous of anyone? How to live with detachment? Naranbhai Siju says, "When someone is born we celebrate, but when someone passes on, we grieve – why should that be the case? One should not live with extremities but do everything with moderation." Naranbhai ends the conversation on this poignant note, "You must not starve your body, but you must not eat too much as well."[60]

Vankar Bhimji Velji, a Brahmin weaver in Sarli in Kutch is tying the weaver's knot, working on the cemented floor that helps in cooling his body through the afternoon heat. Once a warp has been entirely woven and off the loom, *taana* (new warp) is manually joined to the beam, one thread at a time. During this process, the taana regularly slips, because the weaver sweats a lot. In total, there are 2100–2200 *taar* (individual warp threads) which collectively take up a lot of time. A tiny mistake can create a glaring gap. When I arrived at his workshop, Bhimji was singing a song while tying these knots. When I asked what he was singing, he chuckled "*Bas man marzi se, mazak mazak mei*" (Just made something on my own, for some fun). Upon further probing, he shared the song he drafted while performing the knotting operation – "*Ye dhaaga kata, ye dhaaga joda*" (Here I cut the yarn, here I join another).

Bhimji very succinctly explains through one of Kabir's couplet how it helps him maintain concentration while working:

Kabir teri jhopdi gal katiyan ke paas
Karega so bharega, Kabir tu kyu rahe udaas?

'One who sows, he shall reap' – a person will get results in life, in accordance with his deeds.

He continues, "Now there are 2000 threads here, if my mind gets distracted, then I will not be able to concentrate." He follows up with another couplet that discusses how one's senses are continually distracted.

> *Kabir Kabir kya kaho, khojo aap shareer*
> *Paanch indrayi vash karo, khud aap Kabir.*
>
> (Think about your body and learn to control your five sesnses)

Like him, many of the weavers in Bhujodi are active singers in *mandilis* (regional gatherings of musicians). Not only as organised groups but every evening before dinner, weavers practice their music within their families, as part of what they call a *kirtan*.[61] A Kabir scholar, Linda Hess defines kirtan as "a live performance where physical bodies are interacting, and where sounds are produced by singers and heard by listeners who are present in the same place at the same time."[62] An hour-long familial performance, my friend and I invited ourselves to one such kirtan at Bhimji's house one evening and it was nothing short of a meditative experience. Everybody was found draped in a Kutchi shawl woven by the men and finished by the women of the house. With eyes shut and bodies taut, like an imaginary thread, they chanted and sang praises of Narayan, Ramakrishna and Rahim.

Premji shares how *mann* (soul) is the *raja* (king) of everything and how it should be devoid of any *kubudhi* (foolishness). He adds,

> "The thread of truth runs through your entire body; material things superimpose this thread. If you hold the correct thread of life, all the other things will disappear. If dispassion takes root inside, then you cannot work. You should not move from where you stand."

Premji's wisdom was layered with an old popular Bollywood song echoing in the courtyard of his house – *Zindagi kaisi hai paheli* (What a riddle life is).

He goes on to explain some of Kabir's bhajans which because of his age, he had a hard time recalling the verses:

> *Tap ki tur na bhi lagayi, smaran sachi batayi*
> *Dharam ka doori baaju mei lagayi, tur par taani lagayi*
>
> *Hardam madhero lagayi, uske dhaaga mei dhaaga lagayi*
> *Pawan pawano milayi, challan lagi, Ram rachaiya lagayi*
>
> *Khyal nu khutu khat se khodo, vyagar vadar lagayi*
> *Tab hui meri pachtayi.*
>
> (Even if I didn't do penance, I told him to remember the truth.
> I put the religion aside and put a stop.

I always put my head in the thread, I put thread in the thread.
The wind mixed the winds, the movement started, Ram created it.
Don't worry, dig deeper, apply pressure.
Then I regretted it.)

The verses contained a lot of terms related to thread and various parts of the loom as well as the action of weaving. For instance, *duriya* is the wooden pole located at both ends of the loom and *tur* is the beam on which *taana* (wrap) is wound. "*Uske dhaaga mei dhaaga lagayi*" translates to the act of tying the weaver's knot.

As many there are nerves in the body, the body is thus referred to as a collection of threads. While many songs are laden with the recurring leitmotif of warp and weft and the loom, charkha too figures as a poetic simile; how one creates their entire body from a loom or a charkha. *Mera charkha bole ram tuhi tuhi* – while working on the loom, whatever the weaver felt inside, they made a loom or a charkha of their body.[63]

Ranaji shares a part of Kabir's quatrain,

Charkhe wali naar
Tun tun karte taar
Charkhe ka bedh batao
Kaatand wali naar.

Here, the charkha is representative of one's life, Ranaji translates it for me. Directing his finger to an imaginary charkha he says, "this charkha that I crafted from my life". *Taar* means the thread being spun on the charkha but here it is employed as a metaphor to represent the face. The charkha that is moving is actually the breath moving. He says charkha runs on *mann* (soul), the *taar* then becomes one's way of thinking. When one puts their focus on the taar, it will continue to spin because the thread is imbued with the breath.[64]

As Purshottam Agrawal concurs, this 'Bhakti', or emotional response to the divine in the form of bhajans, is part of most of the religions and finds expression in rituals and poetry of adoration.[65] What has been discussed here is only one of the many types of vocal music practised in Kutch. Some men also sing *maulud*, which translates as 'prayer' in Arabic and the singing is performed without any musical instruments.[66] Muslim Maldharis are known to sing *kafi kalam*, an expressive music similar to Sufi and sung in praise of the divine.[67]

Bhamal Jaimalji's performing group, 'Bhanu Bhagat Bhujodi Mandali' is over fifty years old. Today, many weavers hold an active presence on YouTube. Jaimalji was an erstwhile weaver but has now left the loom as of October 2023. The loom lies deserted in the middle of the barren, sandy courtyard of his house. When I enquired after it, he went and sat in the pit and imitated the action of weaving on the abandoned loom – how he used to weave. He now works for a Multi-National Corporation (MNC) on a night shift at a construction site because apparently, the surrounding area receives a lot of robbery cases.

Case Study 2: Naranbhai Siju Mandan

Naranbhai Siju learnt to weave in 1992 and wove shawls as a job worker for 20–25 years. He tried to establish a shawl-weaving business but failed twice. Facing tough competition, he moved to a carpet-weaving business. In 2008, his son finished a design course at Kala Raksha Vidhyalaya and began creating new designs.[68] He got his products marketed widely and with an encouraging push from organisations such as Khamir, the business transitioned to a thriving enterprise today.

Naranbhai is a known figure in Bhujodi for his knowledge of Kabir's bhajans. He maintains an active YouTube channel as a way of preserving this *sanskruti* (culture). But he was not a bhajan singer always. He shares how it was only in 2007 when filmmaker and artist Shabnam Virmani visited the village and created a documentary titled 'ad anarth' that something clicked for Naranbhai after watching it. An *adhyatmik* (spiritual) understanding dawned upon him. He delved deeper and started practising the bhajans, referring to them as *manthan-chintan* (churning-contemplation within). He sat with the elders, attended bhajans at other people's homes and soon built his own repertoire of songs.

Slowly, when he owned a phone, he began recording wherever he heard these songs and would later listen to them. That is how he developed this expansive knowledge. He does not sing individually, but only in a chorus group of mandilis. This is, he says, the inhabitants' way of maintaining their *parampara* (tradition). As a way of serving his community, he does not charge a fee for singing in any of the mandilis when he is invited; he only charges for his travel.

In my conversation with him, Naranbhai revealed the hidden niceties of these bhajans. He sang a few and elaborated on the underlying meaning. He started with one of the most popular songs '*Kayawadi mei sootar samjhayee liye*'. *Sootar* means cotton thread and *vaadi* is a garden. The song loosely translates as how one's body and its feelings are continually distracted, being constantly entangled in material and immaterial things. Amidst all of this, the thread in the form of life has to be disentangled, kept in a straight imaginary line. If one sees beyond the surface, there is an integration of the fundamental Pythagoras' theorem within this song. The arrangement of threads akin to that on the loom has to be positioned at 90 degrees which holds true for the mind's concentration as well – it has to be aligned at the right angle. "That life would be perfect where the soul does not deviate much", adds Naranbhai.

There are thousands of songs like these, many that Naranbhai himself has not set his ears on yet. "Everything is one absolute truth. If we have got a life, then death is a definite fact", he says. Songs are structured around the events of one's life, for instance, different bhajans are sung while grieving. "Mere singing is not enough, one has to feel and sing", he adds. He discussed how bhajans have the power to evoke *karuna* (compassion) in the singer. Many weavers still find it challenging to understand the layered meanings within these bhajans, before they begin to internalise them.

Some weavers can still be found murmuring verses while working on the loom. It has become a way of developing concentration and nothing else could dare enter their minds once the bhajan surfaces on their lips, deemed all the more important in a world that is increasingly becoming distracting. However, weavers no longer craft their own songs like Bhimji did in front of me. They are unable to use the lyrical world of songs to articulate their inner feelings; it is a rarity to find a weaver who does.

Conclusion

I remember a part of Kabir's couplet from my sixth grade Hindi lesson at school, the meaning of which, I only learnt much later in life,

> *Pal mei pralay hoyegi, bahuri karoge kab.*
>
> (In a moment of apocalypse, heads whirl, afraid of the future, they howl at the past).[69]

In the last two decades, Kutch has transformed into a prosperous hub that attracts tourists from the world over, as much for its crafts as for the annual cultural festival Rannotsav held on the pristine white grounds of the Rann. The Meghwals have benefitted financially from this exposure, placing them higher on the social ladder. Bhujodi is one of the weaving clusters in India, where the number of looms has increased, instead of decreasing; from 50–100 a decade ago to 150–200 active looms at present.

The weaver receives a better wage as well, albeit meagre when compared to other professions. A weaver's daily wage in Bhujodi ranges from 800 to 1000 INR today. Compared to a weaver's pay in Bengal which ranges from 150 to 250, this wage is four-fold! Hamirji Vishram shares how comparatively, the *taraiwala* (the person who applies plaster on the wall before applying paint) makes a minimum of 1200 INR a day.

Notwithstanding the low wages, the significantly 'better' pay of the weaver is reflected in how expensive Kutch has become over the years.

Interestingly, the measure of an area's cost of living can be deduced from the cost of essentials such as salt and sugar, as Hamirji mentioned and he soon started asking me the price of *khaand* (sugar) in Bengal and Kerala. "Everyone needs a Honda [car] here", he retorts, discussing how high weavers aspire now. This prosperity of the region has incurred a reverse migration where people are moving to Bhujodi and learning to weave like Umaid Shree Bhai or Bhimji Velji.

From woollen shawls to the Bhujodi sari, the shifting climate has resulted in a shift in styles too. Duplicate shawls are now being manufactured in Ludhiana and shipped to Kutch and other parts of Western India.[70] Surprisingly, the weaving of the much-famed 'Bhujodi Sari' is a relatively new phenomenon in Kutch. Namori Kaka discussed how saris came much later to Bhujodi, in 1950, when a Gandhian leader's wife wore the first khadi sari ever woven by a weaver in the village. It is also known that the traditional women's drape in Kutch, the *khombi*, akin to an *odhani*, evolved into a sari later.[71] Paired with a *ghagra* (skirt), another older version of *khombi* was the *putaara*. This nomenclature for the craft is not fair as well because as discussed in the previous sections, there are other villages in and around Bhujodi where the same weaving technique is practised. What this leads to then is a monopolisation of the market, resulting in inequalities among the Vankars. Regrettably, it was only on my fifth visit that I discovered these weavers beyond Bhujodi.

Where weavers in other clusters across the country have moved to weaving with extra weft by installing a jacquard box above their looms, designs in Kutch are still hand-crafted assiduously by the weaver's fingers. Despite this, the diaphanous jamdani sari attracts more customers than the colourful Kutchi weave sari. Shamji Vishram gave a rationale for this distinction, as discussed earlier in this chapter too, how the recognition of a textile is dependent on the end buyer in addition to the visual appeal of the textile.

The sentience of Kutch's inhabitants and their attentiveness to their immediate environment cannot escape anyone who comes and interacts with them. Further, in the double performative act of singing while weaving, the weavers' many interrogations with the self were uncovered. The learning that Vankars of Bhujodi are poets and singers too is a riveting thought to deliberate on as to when the weaver becomes the poet and the poet becomes the weaver. Knowing the weavers as *Kabirpanthis* and how Kabir's songs have been adapted and sung by them is evocative of how textile-making affords a way for knowing one's very being.[72] Much to my disappointment, I could not discover any reference in the bhajans to either spinning or the desi oon. Also, only men in Kutch sing while women are known to sing other kinds of songs.

Notes

1 Shamji Vishram, personal communication, January 2, 2024.
2 Umaid Shree Bhai, personal communication, Bhujodi, January 1, 2024.
3 Premji Velji Siju, personal communication, January 4, 2024.
4 An admixture of Gujarati, Sindhi and Marwari, Kutchi is a script-free language.
5 Rita Kothari, *Memories and Movements: Borders and Communities in Banni Kutch, Gujarat* (New Delhi: Orient BlackSwan, 2013), 2.
6 Archana Shah, *Shifting Sands. Kutch: Textiles Traditions, Transformations* (India: Bandhej Books, 2013), 30.
7 Shah, *Shifting Sands*, 25.
8 Siddharth Mangariya, personal communication, January 1, 2024.
9 Namori Kaka, personal communication, January 3, 2024.
10 Siddharth Mangariya, personal communication, January 1, 2024.
11 A starching worker in Bhujodi, personal communication, January 3, 2024.
12 Anjali Karolia, *Traditional Indian Handcrafted Textiles: History, Techniques, Process, Designs Vol II Woven Textiles* (New Delhi: Niyogi Books, 2019), 57.
13 Vankar Poonam Arjan, personal communication, January 5, 2024.
14 Namori Kaka, personal communication, January 3, 2024; Vankar Poonam Arjan, personal communication, January 5, 2024.
15 Siddharth Mangariya, personal communication, January 1, 2024.
16 Shamji Vishram, personal communication, January 2, 2024.
17 Namori Kaka, personal communication, January 3, 2024.
18 Shamji Vishram, personal communication, January 2, 2024.
19 Shah, *Shifting Sands*, 68.
20 Siddharth Mangariya, personal communication, January 1, 2024.
21 Namori Kaka, personal communication, January 3, 2024.
22 Namori Kaka, personal communication, January 3, 2024.
23 Shamji Vishram, personal communication, January 2, 2024.
24 Bhamal Jaimalji, personal communication, January 5, 2024. For a detailed study on the infiltration and popularity of Bt Cotton in Indian fields, see Archana Shah, *Crafting a Future: Stories of Indian Textiles and Sustainable Practices* (New Delhi: Niyogi Books, 2021), 102–103.
25 Shamji Vishram, personal communication, January 2, 2024.
26 Naranbhai Siju, personal communication, January 3, 2024.
27 Namori Kaka, personal communication, January 3, 2024.
28 Siddharth Mangariya, personal communication, January 1, 2024.
29 Ranaji, personal communication, January 4, 2024
30 Naranbhai Siju, personal communication, January 3, 2024.
31 Indian Trade Portal, 'Wool and Woolen Textile from India', https://www.indiantradeportal.in/vs.jsp?lang=0&id=0,31,24100,24124
32 Bhamal Jaimalji, personal communication, January 5, 2024.
33 Naranbhai Siju, personal communication, January 3, 2024.

34 Other pastoralist communities of Gujarat include Bharvad (grazers of sheep and goats), Rabari, (keepers of camels), Charan (keeper of buffaloes and bullocks), Ahir (keepers of cows) and Maldharis (keepers of cattle).
35 Shamji Vishram, personal communication, January 2, 2024.
36 Judy Frater, "Warp and Weft: Tradition and Change, Craftsmen and Innovation in Bhujodi." *Marg* 73, no. 4 (2022): 130–135.
37 One *haath* measures approximately 15 inches.
38 Richard Critchfield, *Villages* (New York: Anchor Books, 1983), 126.
39 Naranbhai Siju, personal communication, January 3, 2024.
40 Namori Kaka, personal communication, January 3, 2024.
41 Shashi Tharoor discusses this in an article. See "Caste consciousness is greater today than in the 1950s: Tharoor." The Times of India, November 12, 2022. https://timesofindia.indiatimes.com/india/caste-consciousness-is-greater-today-than-in-1950s-tharoor/articleshow/95475917.cms?utm_source=contentofinterest&utm_medium=text&utm_campaign=cppst.
42 Hamirji Vishram, personal communication, January 1, 2024.
43 Robin Wall Kimmerer, *Braiding Sweetgrass: Indigenous Wisdom, Scientific Knowledge and the Teachings of Plants* (UK: Penguin Books, 2020), 115.
44 Earthquake is a common reference point for the inhabitants of Kutch. Hamirji Vishram, personal communication, January 1, 2024.
45 Shah, *Crafting a Future*, 217.
46 Alexander Langlands, *Craeft: An Enquiry into the Origins and True Meaning of Traditional Crafts* (New York: Norton, 2018), 340.
47 Siddharth Mangariya, personal communication, January 1, 2024.
48 Naranbhai Siju, personal communication, January 3, 2024.
49 Vankar Poonam Arjan, personal communication, January 5, 2024.
50 Shah, *Shifting Sands*.
51 Walter Isaacson, *Steve Jobs* (New York: Simon and Schuster, 2011), 48.
52 Umaid Shree Bhai, personal communication, January 1, 2024.
53 Vijaya Ramaswamy, *The Song of the Loom: Weaver Folk Traditions in South India* (India, Kundli: Primus Books, 2013), 4.
54 Lucy Norris, "Creating Fame and Fortune from the Ruins of Handloom in Kerala, Southern India," *Textile Economies: Power and Value from the Local to the Transitional. Alta Mir, Lantham* (2011): 285–305.
55 Lambros Malafouris and Maria-Danae Koukouti, "Where the touching is touched: The role of haptic attentive unity in the dialogue between maker and material," *Multimodality & Society* 2, no. 3 (2022): 265–287.
56 Bruce Metcalf, "Craft and Art, Culture and Biology," In *The Culture of Craft*, edited by Peter Dormer, 67–83 (Manchester: Manchester University Press, 1997), 75.
57 Ramaswamy, *The Song of the Loom*.
58 Shah, *Shifting Sands*, 222.
59 Agrawal, *Kabir Kabir*, 52.

60 Naranbhai Siju, personal communication, January 3, 2024.
61 The system is often a joint family set-up instead of a nuclear one.
62 Linda Hess, *Bodies of Song: Kabir Oral Traditions and Performative Worlds in North India* (New York: Oxford University Press, 2015), 9.
63 Naranbhai Siju, personal communication, January 3, 2024.
64 Ranaji, personal communication, January 4, 2024.
65 Purushottam Agrawal, *Kabir, Kabir: The Life and Work of Early Modern Poet-Philosopher* (Chennai: Westland Non-Fiction, 2021), 5.
66 Shah, *Shifting Sands*, 19.
67 Shah, *Shifting Sands*, 139.
68 Kala Raksha Vidhyalaya is an educational institution that works with the artisans of Kutch in skill training and capacity building.
69 Translation by Shabnam Virmani. See See Virmani, “TEDxDelhi”.
70 Namori Kaka, personal communication, January 3, 2024.
71 Namori Kaka, personal communication, January 3, 2024.
72 Betty Risteen Hasselkus, *The Meaning of Everyday Occupation* (NJ, Thorofare: Slack, 2002), 17.

Bibliography

Agrawal, Purushottam. *Kabir, Kabir: The Life and Work of the Early Modern Poet-Philosopher*. Chennai: Westland Non-Fiction, 2021.

Critchfield, Richard. *Villages*. New York: Anchor Books, 1983.

Frater, Judy. “Warp and Weft: Tradition and Change, Craftsmen and Innovation in Bhujodi.” *Marg* 73, no. 4 (2022): 130–135.

Hasselkus, Betty Risteen. *The Meaning of Everyday Occupation*. NJ, Thorofare: Slack, 2002.

Hess, Linda. *Bodies of Song: Kabir Oral Traditions and Performative Worlds in North India*. New York: Oxford University Press, 2015.

Isaacson, Walter. *Steve Jobs*. New York: Simon and Schuster, 2011.

Kimmerer, Robin Wall. *Braiding Sweetgrass: Indigenous Wisdom, Scientific Knowledge and the Teachings of Plants*. UK: Penguin Books, 2020.

Karolia, Anjali. *Traditional Indian Handcrafted Textiles: History, Techniques, Process, Designs Vol II Woven Textiles*. New Delhi: Niyogi Books, 2019.

Kothari, Rita. *Memories and Movements: Borders and Communities in Banni Kutch, Gujarat*. New Delhi: Orient BlackSwan, 2013.

Langlands, Alexander. *Craeft: An Enquiry into the Origins and True Meaning of Traditional Crafts*. New York: Norton, 2018.

Malafouris, Lambros and Maria-Danae Koukouti. “Where the Touching is Touched: The Role of Haptic Attentive Unity in the Dialogue between Maker and Material.” *Multimodality & Society* 2, no. 3 (2022): 265–287.

Metcalf, Bruce. “Craft and Art, Culture and Biology.” In *The Culture of Craft*, edited by Peter Dormer, 67–83. Manchester: Manchester University Press, 1997.

Norris, Lucy. "Creating Fame and Fortune from the Ruins of Handloom in Kerala, Southern India." In *Textile Economies: Power and Value from the Local to the Transitional*, 285–305. Lantham: Alta Mir, 2011.

Ramaswamy, Vijaya. *The Song of the Loom: Weaver Folk Traditions in South India*. India, Kundli: Primus Books, 2013.

Shah, Archana. *Shifting Sands. Kutch: Textiles, Traditions, Transformations*. Bandhej Books, 2013.

Shah, Archana. *Crafting a Future: Stories of Indian Textiles and Sustainable Practices*. New Delhi: Niyogi Books, 2021.

7 The Kasavu Textiles of Kuthampully Handloom Village

> "Weaving does not have to be in your blood, if you are willing to learn, you can learn to weave in just three months."[1]

In a small village neighbouring the town of Thiruvilwamala, in the state of Kerala in South India, one wakes up to the sound of the handloom. Staying here in a weaver's house that was nearly a hundred years old, the weaving in the adjacent room would begin as early as 6 am. Usually, the weavers in the village could be found at their looms as early as 5 am too, working well into the night till about 8 pm. This is often coupled with an afternoon siesta of 2–3 hours which becomes particularly essential during hot afternoons, throughout the year. Even in the relatively cooler months of December and January, it becomes necessary to pause work for a while.

The weaving community in Kuthampully are largely the Devangas, a concatenation of the words '*deva's angas*,' (the deities' clothes) who are Brahmins hailing from the Mysore region in the present-day state of Karnataka. The community's main goddess is Chamundeshwari and so the belief goes that the weavers are actually weaving *angis* (garments) for the deities.[2] Nearly 500 years ago, upon the invitation of the Maharaja of Kochi, the Devangas migrated from their original lands (at the time under Tipu Sultan's reign) to the region that is now Kerala. However, in the absence of any confirmed evidence, this narrative is often considered ahistorical by the Devangas themselves and is contested by the lore that the Kochi Maharaja himself required clothing which is why he made the Devanga weavers settle here.[3] One of the weavers wove cloth for the lady of the royal family of Kochi which became highly desirable and that is how the cluster became established. In this manner, the royal family were the primaeval wearers of the handwoven fabric that Kuthampully produces today, albeit the numbers are receding, as this chapter discusses.

There are two rivers, Gayathripuzah and Bharathappuzha that traverse through Kuthampully. With a generous collective water flow, the soil

DOI: 10.4324/9781003450061-7

around the river gets eroded regularly which has made the land gradually steeper. In Malayalam '*kuttane*' means steep and '*kulli alegal*' means rice or paddy, so the land where rice paddy is grown is called 'Kuthampully' and that is how the village derived its name.[4] There is yet another story where the name Kuthampully means 'sit here' and since the migrant weavers eventually settled here, the village was christened such.[5]

Where the current population of Kuthampully once neared 5000, in the present day, there are no more than 200–300 weavers in the village. This number is problematic since there are no existing records or census to verify. Weavers and traders differ in the numbers they postulate, and as per one, the present count even touched 500! While the number of looms is usually used as a reference point to tally up the number of weavers in the village, this is however, erroneous since most of the looms are either inactive or the pits have been filled in.[6] The latter was observed as a regular feature in many workplaces where one or more pits had been covered up. These closings of pits are symbolic of how rapidly handloom weaving is ceasing as part of this culture.

Apart from Devangas, there are weavers hailing from outside the village who make up 10% of the weaving community in Kuthampully. These weavers come from neighbouring areas or from the adjacent state of Tamil Nadu. Identifying themselves as Malayalis some of them are hereditary weavers whereas others have taken to weaving only much recently. The landscape of Kuthampully is thus a mix of independent houses that weavers work out of or separate weaving sheds where the weavers work as a collective. Within the workspace, the organisation of the weaving spaces differed too. Although the house and the working space seamlessly exist within the same small area, the surroundings are kept spartan including the space around the loom (Figure 7.1). There is also ample ventilation with open windows and passageways that facilitate the ease of working. When compared to other clusters in India, the sound of looms reverberates differently in Kuthampully, being felt slightly faster than in other regions. It sounded smoother and more rhythmic; maybe this was so since no extra wefts were involved in weaving a plain kasavu that would have otherwise broken the rhythm.

The Weave becomes the Brand

A pristine white, translucent body finished with a gold kasavu border running along the two parallel edges, the Kasavu Sari is a regional textile that Kuthampully is renowned for. It now forms an important part of every woman's wedding trousseau in Kerala.[7] Considered auspicious, a new kasavu sari is worn during ceremonies, temple rituals and festivals such as Onam and Vishu.[8] In fact, weavers pace up and weave faster when festivals, especially Onam, are approaching.[9] However, the sari was not always

Figure 7.1 A kasavu sari in making.

woven in Kuthampully and was not a traditional attire that Kerala women wore. It was the *thorthu* (towel), *mundu* (a man's drape for the lower body) and *settu mundu* (a two-piece woman's drape) that were woven traditionally, the sari became popular only much later due to a surge in demand.

Kerala has never been a sari-wearing state and it is only in the last thirty years or so that the drape has gained this increased prominence in the region. It is ironic that Kuthampully received the Geographical

Indication (GI) tag for its jacquard-woven saris that are not even traditional to the region, unlike *thorthu* or *mundu*![10] Prabhu, owner of Asha Handlooms (a popular stop in Kuthampully for tourists and textile connoisseurs alike), justifies this tag by mentioning how the village's uniqueness is in the sari woven using the jacquard mechanism that renders elaborate designs on the *pallav*. Demonstrative of the virtuosity of the weavers, it is not just the end product, the sari with a jacquard pallav, but the process that is unique. For instance, a narrow temple motif detail on both ends of the pallav, called *chutti*, a subtle marker of the threshold where the body of the sari ends and the pallav begins, is considered a distinguished skill of the handloom weaver. When placed next to each other, the difference between a power loom and a handloom textile can barely be spotted save for the *chutti* which can only be replicated on the power loom as a crude version. While there are no visible differences between the textiles woven on the two looms, handloom is still known for better quality and breathability of the textile, allowing easy passage of the air.[11]

This being my second visit to the region, I could already notice the changes from when I had last visited nearly five years ago. As soon as one enters the village, the landscape is dotted with hoardings and signages pointing to various 'Handloom Textile' retail and wholesale shops, with newer hoardings sprouting between my two visits. Beginning with names such as Rama, Sudha or Supriya, the businesses are named after the owner's sisters or daughters. The weavers' homes and traders' shops co-existed in the village with a strange paradox visible when one moves deeper into the interiors. There can barely be found any handloom textiles at these 'Handloom' shops even though the inhabitants undertake only handloom weaving. There is no power loom to be found in the village, while on the contrary, there are only power loom textiles stocked at these shops and selling as 'handloom'. As was soon found, the shops give orders to industries in Tamil Nadu and procure power loom textiles from them to be eventually sold in Kuthampully. At present, there are over 120 such shops in the entire village.[12]

Kuthampully has evolved differently when compared to other weaving clusters across the country, where power looms have taken over. Like Bhujodi in Kutch, there could be found no power looms, primarily because it leads to sound pollution. So even if one were to keep a power loom, the neighbours would obstruct and not permit it in order to maintain the village ecology.[13] In addition to the community's collective resistance, there were labour issues as well with limited people ready to look after or manage the looms.[14] For instance, Somu Sarees, a prime retailer in Kuthampully, was earlier running 14–15 looms, but in post-pandemic times, they were forced to shut all of them down.[15]

Over the decades, Kuthampully has become a brand in itself. It has become merely a denotative of a regional textile that rarely gets sold in the village. Because the market has already been established, there is the added advantage of selling power loom saris in Kuthampully. While this has led to the prosperity of traders with an increase in weaver-turned-traders, it is still tricky because the power loom saris (including the new trend of painted or printed saris) are sold under the façade of Kuthampully, a misleading representation of a handloom village. With a whopping twenty million rupees worth of textile market annually, the handloom products still constitute only 10% of the sales from the village.[16]

The traders constitute a growing group of retailers and wholesalers in Kuthampully. They procure raw materials from various parts of the country and hand them over to the weavers. There are looms as well that are given out by the traders to migrant weavers. These traders are not first-generation traders, in many cases even their grandfathers did not know how to weave and neither do the present traders' children, although they belong to the Devanga community. The traders, apart from selling through their retail shops in the village, also sell at major shops in the cities in South India such as Pothys and Seematti. One such prime trader, Asha Handlooms stocks both handloom and power loom textiles. They work with nearly fifty individual weavers and other work sheds in Kuthampully.[17] While conducting interviews with the traders, there was found an underlying oblivion, a kind of detachment from the weavers' present state and conditions.

It is unfortunate that a trader's job is considered a sign of prestige unlike a weaver's. A job at the bank is considered better than weaving since it offers better prospects.[18] Many weavers have now moved from weaving to a trading practice resulting in traders outnumbering the weavers in Kuthampully. Where earlier weavers suffered more hardships, barely managing two complete meals a day, the economic situation is considered far better now.[19]

With shifting trends, the kasavu sari has become symbolic of the traditional attire of Kerala. A lot of textiles thus get exported from Kuthampully all over the world, wherever Keralites reside.[20] As per Prabhu's observations, people are very comfortable in the village and are comparatively more lethargic than weavers in other clusters in India.[21] Nevertheless, even though a weaver works harder, he gets paid less than a trader which entails less labour-intensive work.

Traditional Processes and Weather Conditions

In Kuthampully, many of the traditional processes around weaving are community-oriented, requiring collaboration between individuals and families. One such process is Street Warping which has nearly disappeared from other weaving clusters in India. This protracted practice can still be witnessed each morning on the streets and lanes of Kuthampully wherein not just the family members but the entire village participates to help prepare each other's warp.

Historian Prasannan Parthasarathi writes how earlier, weavers in South India were primarily agriculturalists who would undertake spinning and weaving during times of drought when agricultural activities would cease or there was little chance of a good yield.[22] By the late nineteenth century, spinning had nearly vanished from South Indian villages. Similarly, Street Sizing, a traditional process of starching the yarn, used to be performed till about thirty years ago.[23] Being undertaken in an open area, under the sun, it relied heavily on the weather, requiring an ideal temperature of 15–20°C. It should not be too sunny – one had to finish the laborious process before the sun was out. Further, as a region that receives good bouts of monsoon, rains in Kuthampully would play havoc often, increasing the time the warp takes to dry completely. At times, the entire warp used to get destroyed, with the weaver sitting idle with nothing to weave, which incurred heavy losses for him. This was an issue in earlier times when the monsoon season was longer.

"Doing street sizing is hell-like! When it would rain, the scenario was akin to starvation earlier, no work means no wages", one of the traders agonised over.[24] Nearly 25 years back, yarns were sourced from Coimbatore in Tamil Nadu, the river body was used to stamp and clean the yarn and later street sizing was performed next to it. This system was discontinued owing to its laborious nature and propitious weather conditions that were essential.[25] Instead, the yarn when now purchased from the market, comes starched in bundles called *pavu*. Because the process of street sizing is nearly extinct in the region, for the weaver it is little concerning if it rains less or more.[26]

Out of the 300 active looms in Kuthampully, half of them are pit looms. The pit loom was deemed perfect for South Indian weavers since they were often on the move and the loom itself was relatively light and simple to assemble and disassemble.[27] A further advantage of the pit loom was that the dug ground created the right level of humid conditions for cotton weaving that prevented the yarn from regular snapping or getting brittle.[28] A missionary intervention by the German Basel Mission, the Malabar frame looms (that came with a wider frame) later replaced the pit looms. Also called raised-pit looms or stand looms, a platform is constructed ground up for the weaver to sit comfortably, appearing as if customised for every individual weaver. While earlier, the loom was set up inside the mud house, nowadays a detachable version of the loom is available. Now, even if one has a smaller space, a loom could be set up while earlier more space was required to set up the pit loom. Fly shuttle was introduced in the region fifty years ago; nobody at present works with a throw shuttle.

One cannot talk about climate change without talking about sustainable practices, revealing evidence of a circular economy that once was the norm. As with other weaving villages in India, almost all the parts of the tree were used in the construction of the house. In Kuthampully too, the ceiling was earlier crafted out of palm leaves which kept the house cool during summers. However, they did not last long and during the rainy season, they would fall off.[29] Decades ago, the thick branch of *thailam* leaf was cut and used as bobbins instead of the plastic ones in use today, however, they would only last the weaver two weeks and thus had to be continually replaced. This tree no longer grows across the river, where it used to once thrive.[30] Leaves of the teak tree were used by shopkeepers to wrap meat and fish. Where plastic has now infiltrated the very interiors of the village and with a lack of proper disposal systems in place, unlike in the cities, there is regular burning of plastic waste that proves detrimental to the village environs.[31]

The Weather and the Weaver

Referred to as *kaalavastha* in Malayalam, climate change in Kuthampully was found to have little effect on the daily life of weavers. On the contrary, as the interviews revealed, the change has been for the better. While this sentiment was echoed by most of the weavers, as conversations progressed and upon further probing finer nuances were uncovered. As per the weavers, there are no serious issues although change can be discernibly felt. Here, contrary to the previous two case studies, the effects of the climate resulted in a positive change which has got to do more with the shifting weaving landscape of Kuthampully itself.

Prabhu mentions how climate change affects agriculturalists the most. In late 2023, nearly all the paddy fields were destroyed due to unexpected rain. Till about 10–15 years ago, paddy cultivation was actively practised in the area next to the river but it ceased to exist because it was not reaping any profit. At present, nothing is cultivated in the village, except for coconut, while outside the village, there can still be found some rice-growing areas.

Tropical climate is considered an ideal climate for weaving – a little bit of humidity, a little bit of moisture, not too high temperature, and not too low as well. The January weather is deemed favourable for weaving while during summer, the weaver is himself tired from the torpid heat. The textile business thus runs for six months only – six months of production coupled with six months of sale. During the Onam season, heavy rainfall surfaces which proves disadvantageous in terms of production; the weavers and traders have to plan the stock earlier. For the last 3–4 years, the change has been more observable. The weavers have reoriented and found the best time to work in the wee hours of the morning from 5 to 9 am and then in the evening between 4 and 6 pm.

Kerala receives the tropical monsoon and where earlier it used to rain beginning the first of June, that is not the case anymore. Prabhu mentions how there used to be *pukka* rain (a hard monsoon) when he was young. But for the last 5–6 years, Kuthampully has received a delayed monsoon each year, with unpredictable and irregular rains. Further, the rainy season has shrunk now. This unpredictability of the monsoon poses problems for the weavers, because while undertaking street warping, one has to be mindful of operating at a certain speed, lest there is a sudden downpour, they are able to wrap up the process quickly.[32]

Earlier, when it would rain, all work would be paused – the weavers would sit idle. Now, as Vasudevsan says, it does not matter how or when it rains. Barring the loss of a climate-sensitive traditional process such as street sizing, rains do not bother weavers anymore.[33] Less rain is in fact deemed to be a good thing for processes undertaken in the open air such as street warping.[34]

Prolonged rains that used to last weeks brought various structural issues with the movement of parts of the loom. Owing to increased moisture in the air, the wood of the loom swells up which creates increased friction at the pedal joints, thereby increasing the chances of yarn breakage. The pedal becomes tight to press on, becoming heavier with wood expansion that demands extra bodily force to be applied. At times, it even gets stuck requiring the weaver to repeatedly get down and fix it or warm it up for a smoother operation. Particularly for the elderly, it is more troubling. The weaver population of Kuthampully is largely constituted of older weavers. As has been the case with many other weaving families in India, the next generation is showing little interest in becoming involved with the craft. In fact, the youngest weaver in Kuthampully was aged 32, at the time when this fieldwork was conducted.

Earlier during heavy rains, the river water would fill up the weavers' pit looms. Now the levels do not rise that much. The flow of the rivers is from South to North, so the pit looms situated near the lower side of Gayathripuzah would get flooded more easily than others. When the calamitous 2018 floods hit Kerala, low-lying areas were flooded, destroying many pit looms in its wake.[35] One weaver narrates that precise moment when he realised his pit was being filled with water. While working on his jacquard loom, Manoharan, whose workspace is located not far from the river, realised at first that there was a snake crawling over but later found that it was the water submerging his feet. Before he knew it, the water had soon reached the level of his knee. At that time the iron needles as part of the jacquard attachment had got rusted, so the entire heddle had to be lifted to prevent further damage. Manoharan has not used his jacquard since then. It lies dormant, lifted high above his loom, the cobwebs having now taken over the jacquard box.

Following an unexpected cloudburst, the 2018 floods in the state happened during the peak Onam season and it took merely three days for the heavy rain to swell up every dam.[36] It is an advantage that the rivers have flowing water, so when floods hit the area, it does not get inundated by an extreme level – the water is not retained in the riparian areas but instead dries up fast.

Akin to a human form, the yarn demands to be kept in a uniform manner. During rains, with increased moisture in the air, cotton flares up which requires more energy on the part of the weaver while beating the fabric. The fraying also creates gaps in the interlacing that require constant fixing to fill them, one thread at a time, so as not to result in an uneven weave.[37] Overall, the efficiency of the weaver during the rainy season is pared back – the increased dampness makes it extremely hard to weave.[38] Even when the rains eventually do stop, the moisture is retained in walls, roofs and other fixtures in the loom.[39] To counteract this, weavers would burn *angeethi* (fire from coal) and place it below the warp so that heat would rise and dry the threads, thereby smoothening the weaving process.[40] This is mainly undertaken in Tamil Nadu; in Kuthampully, weaving with silk is not commonplace and hardly seen. When compared to cotton weaving, silk weaving generates a lot of heat when the weaver ends up spending 8–10 hours on the loom.[41]

Most of the textiles produced within Kuthampully and those sourced from outside are not scientifically stored. During rains, the humid conditions increase the risk of getting the stock destroyed, at times, leaving a white fungus-like residue on the cloth.[42] On the other hand, when it gets extremely hot, the steel racks used for storage heat up as well which necessitates constant air circulation in the storage area. On the contrary, the weaving cluster of Kannur in Kerala, which is renowned for exporting upholstery and home textiles, with government aid, has the provision of a humidity-controlled stock room. Traders or weavers in Kuthampully cannot afford to have such kind of investment. At the moment, for instance, Prabhu has installed heaters and fans to constantly dry the stock when the need arises.

Since weaving is largely undertaken inside the house, the residents are of the view that the practice is less affected by the changing climate although modern houses with an open terrace become much warmer. Prabhu mentions how in earlier times, there were mud houses and mud is known to absorb heat but when it would rain, such houses were considered unsafe owing to regular water leakages.[43] While at present there are still a few old mud houses (100–200 years old) standing in Kuthampully, increasingly many of these are being razed to the ground to create concrete structures.[44] This increases the inside temperature during summer months, significantly impacting the comfort level of the weaver.

A visit to a Self-Help Group (SHG) in Peruvamba village in the Palakkad district in Kerala revealed alternative modes of inhabiting the space around the loom. In a large organised workshed, around thirty weavers could be found working inside. The premises were covered all across with layered asbestos sheets for a rooftop – a material considered carcinogenic for human settlements. It also generates a lot of heat which creates a greenhouse kind of situation when the sun is at its peak. Being the hottest district of Kerala, I could only imagine how heated the shed would be in the summer months.

Looking at the practice of weaving more nuancedly, peak summer also brings with it issues of increased humidity. While working on white is great for ageing eyesight, one has to be careful while weaving with kasavu. Weavers are at an increased risk of sweat releasing from their bodies which stains the kasavu, turning to green or black, owing to the salt content in the sweat. The sweat becomes a way of memorialising the weaver's labour and toil into the textile he is creating. This spot is then considered a defect and the weaver finds it hard to sell the 'damaged' textile because the shops refuse to stock a discoloured textile. Left with no choice, the weaver is forced to sell it at a discounted price. This is the reason why weavers prefer sitting bare-chested while weaving, as it allows for more perspiration.

Changes in Social and Natural Ecology

Over the years, as the number of homes in Kuthampully has been on the increase, weavers feel that the land view has substantially decreased. Bigger trees are declining in numbers, being chopped away to construct new buildings and houses. With plants and trees receding under the disguise of 'development', the avifauna has been impacted as well. While it was refreshing to hear the koel's mellifluous voice while having my morning tea at the stall by the river and getting to spot a kingfisher or two, Prabhu is reminded of how when he was young, there used to be lot many parrots and how it was difficult to spot even a few now. He used to witness cranes seasonally and migratory birds in tens of thousands could be seen every season where there have been none visible for the last decade. Pradeep, a weaver in Kuthampully, adds how the laying of mobile towers in the last 4–5 years has disrupted the village landscape, owing to the emission of strong signals from these towers that have led to birds and squirrels disappearing at an escalating rate. It is only in the last few months when emissions were curbed by the government that those birds can be seen once again.[45]

Pradeep has noticed changes in available fruits and vegetables. For instance, he feels that fruits such as gooseberry and papaya have disappeared from the market; *seetaphal* (custard apple) too is no longer grown in abundance.[46] The 'Communist Tree' (called Jack in the Bush) used to be a great natural source to treat wounds. Pradeep was reminded how when he was a child, if they would get hurt while playing, they would pluck a leaf from this tree and apply it on the wound for quick healing – it was that accessible. The tree has nearly disappeared from the landscape; one will now have to walk far (if one is lucky) to get hold of one such tree.

It is believed that the Devanga weavers settled here in the first place because of the presence of a river. The river water could be utilised for the street sizing process. Prabhu recounts how during his childhood days, he would often go and play in the sand in the evenings. Now a lot of that sand has been removed from the river bank because of construction purposes. The sand serves as a medium to store water and with a reduced soil cover, the groundwater level has gone down as well. It now flows towards the sea which in turn creates a scarcity of water in the area.[47]

The sand alongside the river now serves a different purpose on the handlooms to keep both the warp threads (kasavu and cotton) taut on the loom. This is achieved by hanging weights at the ends, fashioned from sandbags. Even though the two yarns are of different materials, the same pressure needs to be maintained for both to achieve an even weaving. This requires a lot of precision on the weaver's part to create the right balance with separate weights of sand used for kasavu and cotton. Wrapped in bright fabrics like red and fuchsia, these bags in bigger workshops are being replaced with water-filled plastic bottles as seen in the workshed in Palakkad.

As was the case with villages in Kutch, rituals and prayers are imbricated within the weaver's life and work in Kuthampully. Pradeep discusses how he performs a small prayer before he sits on the loom in the morning, and repeats the same while concluding his day. Another weaver Manoharan thinks of lord Ganesa before starting his work. And not just men, women too for instance while performing the process of weaver's knot, do a small prayer before they start.[48] So much interconnected is work with worship that in Devangapuram, another weaving village located 45 kilometres from Kuthampully, a weaver's house had a temple established in the same room where the loom was installed.

Prabhu is also perceptive of how air quality has gradually shifted. With every household in possession of at least three bikes and a minimum of one car, this compounded with every concrete house in the village owning an Air Conditioner (AC), Prabhu feels that the collective emissions have made the air warmer. However, an AC was a rarity in the workplaces I interviewed; a tropical climate is considered ideal for weaving for which constant circulation of air is crucial for both the loom and the fibre.[49]

Screen printing has been a new development in the village, a process that utilises harmful chemical dyes but one that is currently engaging workers in thousands. Creating a pernicious environment for the workers, they are impelled to wear masks to prevent absorption of any noxious fumes. Not only is this damaging to the environment, but it also leads to pollution of water in the wells in the area. The local panchayat cannot put a stop to this practice since many people are involved in the industry and so instead a systematic way of filtering the polluted groundwater has supposedly been put in place.

Case Study 1: Manoharan

55-year-old hereditary weaver, Manoharan sits on his loom where the sun is directly streaming in through a rectangular outlet in the ceiling. It illuminates his body while simultaneously creating a hide-and-seek assemblage with the hanging kasavu. He is wearing a vest because, unlike other weavers, he thinks he does not sweat much. He uses wax to smoothen the yarn where a traditional *maad* is used in Bengal.

Manoharan's workplace was a brick structure, one that would heat up during summers. Next to his loom lay a deserted loom that his wife used to weave on until 2–3 years ago. In fact, till about the 1980s, he used to have as many as six looms. He was employing migrant weavers from Tamil Nadu but owing to the colour identification problem that weavers start facing in their old age, they stopped coming altogether. The loom he is working on is over fifty years old. While the basic structure has remained the same for both a pit loom and a stand loom, the aluminium rod which was earlier made of wood, was frequently changed since it required constant application of pressure.[50] There was a certain wood interlocking system that was traditionally employed where other materials like iron have proved to be long-lasting materials. Wooden looms are evidence of ingenious ways of joining with sturdy interlockings that can withstand movement in the weaving process, thus reflecting their strength and stability.

On discussing with him the now-discontinued process of street sizing, Manoharan recalls how this protracted process was performed before the pavu started coming in the present roll version. There used to be a yarn separator, akin to a big wheel. The weaver used to sit in the pit and the process engaged two or more people. They would later go to the river to clean the yarn, undertake the starching process and then leave it to dry. It was only after following this extensive process that street warping could take place.

Case Study 2: Choundappan

The oldest weaver in the village, Choundappan is 84 years old. His pellucid face could be barely seen from the front of his loom, enmeshed between the alternating strands of cotton and kasavu hanging from the top. Next to the window of the workspace he shares with his son is perched a small table fan that he started using 4–5 years ago. He says how even a small tension in weaving makes him sweat. His bare-chested, portly frame is placed on the loom with a cloth sandwiched in between so as not to let the sweat drip on the loom. Coupled with the fan is the open window that airs his back while also casting the right slant of light on the warp stretched on his loom.

A weaver's common lament is how the warp has a mind of its own that varies with the weather.[51] In the eighteenth century, monsoons used to be intense, so much so that accounts describe how the water kept weavers from their looms with the pits getting filled. Being positioned in the Malabar region, the months of October through March were considered the most suitable to weave since this period was free of any land winds. When severe winds would strike the area, it resulted in the breakage of warp yarns on the loom, taking the weaver additional time to reconnect broken ends, resulting in several knots over the surface of the textile.

In my conversation with Choundappan, an acute observation by him was how the 2007 tsunami altered the wind pattern. He explicates how, prior to the tsunami, harsh winds used to flow, so severely that plants would twist and break and they ended up tying them up quite often, because of which extra work was added to their weaving time. The winds were so strong that yarns used to float and twist during street warping. Now wind patterns have significantly altered which is good for weaving.

For him, by virtue of his age, Choundappan rests extra because he gets tired easily. The work requires him to sleep for 1–2 hours in the noon but he covers this up by working well till 8–9 pm into the night. He adds how his eyesight is all intact and that he can even weave with *karai*, unlike other older weavers. He is of the belief that with the right discipline, one can work anytime, thereby giving weaver the agency. Being habituated to working on the pit loom, neither Choundappan nor his son has moved to a stand loom, unlike other weavers. As my conversations with others revealed, most weavers in Kuthampully do not feel a difference working on either of the looms. Additionally, making a stand loom will entail a cost of at least 15,000 INR whereas a pit loom can be built at half the price. Like other independent weavers in Kuthampully, Choundappan sells to traders in the village itself, the same who also stock power loom textiles from Tamil Nadu.

Conclusion

Prabhu says, "It [Kuthampully] is nice and serene. It is my comfort zone. It is not dusty, there is no pollution and there have been no issues with water shortage or major electricity cuts." Interviews with the traders painted an idealistic image of the village environment with sparse responses about weaver's current conditions. Kuthampully still remains relatively untouched compared to other weaving settlements in East or West India; the weavers here are deemed prosperous.

In contrast, in the village of Devangapuram, the looms are undergoing a slow demise. A visit to the locked quarter that once housed a cooperative society where over 6–8 looms were actively producing handloom fabric, it was now enveloped in foliage, the nature slowly having taken over the remains of human craft, tools and equipment. Witnessing this state of handlooms, one is reminded of the graphic imagery Lucy Norris' article evokes while discussing how deserted cooperatives and sheds have now been taken over by tropical vegetation in Kannur in North Kerala. "Filled with rotting looms, still strung with saggy warps and wefts interlaced with giant cobwebs, suckered creepers, and suspended electrical cables, they once produced handcrafted textiles", she writes.[52]

Today, Kuthampully is a large textile market generating 2.5 billion INR worth of revenue yearly. Handloom products constitute merely 10%, while power loom holds a 90% share. Mismanagement on the part of the village cooperative society has further worsened the situation. There is a traders' association within Kuthampully that weavers are a part of but the government's involvement has been minimal.

If things continue unabated, Prabhu is of the view that by 2030, the industry will succumb. He adds that the very first to vanish from the landscape will be jacquard weavers because they are highly skilled craftsmen and with an ageing population and fewer younger weavers to take over, this skill in particular is at risk since only healthy and physically fit weavers can weave with the jacquard mechanism because of the extra bodily effort and mind-body coordination that the technique demands. As my conversation with Prabhu concludes, even if technology intervention assists, the weaver will have to sit on his loom; weavers are increasingly not choosing to.[53]

Notes

1 Prabhu, personal communication, January 23, 2024.
2 Prabhu, personal communication, January 23, 2024.
3 With a white smear on his wrinkled forehead, Vasudevsan Ramalingam is a 78-year-old temple president and has inherited this title from his ancestors who have been around for nearly 250 years now. He too like other residents of the village, used to weave earlier. Vasudevsan, personal communication, January 26, 2024.
4 I thank Gadha Gopal for this valuable insight, which she discovered through a primary source.
5 Ramalingam, personal communication, January 26, 2024.

6 Manoharan, personal communication, January 24, 2024.
7 It has become a trend now for brides in present times to have one regional textile from across India.
8 60% of the sales for Onam, 25% at the time Vishu and the remaining 15% for marriages and other festivities. Prabhu, personal communication, January 23, 2024.
9 Prabhu, personal communication, January 23, 2024.
10 Although GI hardly affects the market or the sales as Prabhu mentioned, personal communication, January 23, 2024.
11 Anandan, personal communication, January 22, 2024.
12 Anandan, personal communication, January 22, 2024.
13 Rajkumar, personal communication, January 22, 2024.
14 Anandan, personal communication, January 22, 2024.
15 Prabhu, personal communication, January 23, 2024.
16 Prabhu, personal communication, January 23, 2024.
17 A workshed typically has a group of weavers working collectively under the same roof.
18 Rajkumar, personal communication, January 22, 2024.
19 Vasudevsan Ramalingam, personal communication, January 26, 2024.
20 Prabhu, personal communication, January 23, 2024.
21 I think he is seeing it as a trader and as somebody who does not know how to weave. Visiting the other two clusters, I see no difference in this regard.
22 Prasannan Parthasarathi, *The Transition to a Colonial Economy: Weavers, Merchants and Kings in South India, 1720–1800. No. 7* (Cambridge: Cambridge University Press, 2001), 10.
23 This process is still undertaken in the weaving villages of Kutch.
24 Rajkumar, personal communication, January 22, 2024. This is, however, such a contrast to the rain-deprived region of Kutch as discussed in Chapter 6.
25 Anandan, personal communication, January 22, 2024.
26 Anandan, personal communication, January 22, 2024.
27 Parthasarathi, *Transition to Colonial Economy*, 11.
28 Parthasarathi, *Transition to Colonial Economy*, 12.
29 Manoharan, personal communication, January 24, 2024.
30 Choundappan, personal communication, January 27, 2024.
31 Black carbon or soot is believed to have the second-most warming influence on the climate after carbon dioxide. See Veerabhandran Ramanathan and Gregory Carmichael, "Global and Regional Climate Changes due to Black Carbon," *Nature Geoscience* 1, no. 4 (2008): 221–227.
32 Manoharan, personal communication, January 24, 2024.
33 Anandan, personal communication, January 22, 2024.
34 Vasudevsan Ramalingam, personal communication, January 26, 2024.
35 Anandan, personal communication, January 22, 2024.
36 Prabhu, personal communication, January 23, 2024; Rajkumar, personal communication, January 22, 2024.
37 Vasudevsan Ramalingam, personal communication, January 26, 2024.
38 Prabhu, personal communication, January 23, 2024.

39 Pradeep, personal communication, January 23, 2024.
40 Manoharan, personal communication, January 24, 2024.
41 Prabhu, personal communication, January 23, 2024.
42 Rajkumar, personal communication, January 22, 2024.
43 Prabhu, personal communication, January 23, 2024.
44 Prabhu's own childhood mud house was demolished a decade back to construct parking for his shop. Prabhu, personal communication, January 23, 2024.
45 Pradeep, personal communication, January 23, 2024.
46 Prabhu, personal communication, January 23, 2024.
47 Prabhu, personal communication, January 23, 2024.
48 Pradeep, personal communication, January 23, 2024.
49 Anandan mentions that if a house has a terrace, it will have an AC installed. Anandan, personal communication, January 22, 2024.
50 Pradeep, personal communication, January 23, 2024.
51 A similar sentiment is evoked in this paper, see Annapurna Mamidipudi and Wiebe E. Bijker, "Innovation in Indian Handloom Weaving," *Technology and Culture* 59, no. 3 (July 2018): 509–545.
52 Although contextualised in Kannur, Kuthampully is following suit and has undergone a similar phenomenon. See Lucy Norris, "Creating Fame and Fortune from the Ruins of Handloom in Kerala, Southern India," *Textile Economies: Power and Value from the Local to the Transitional* (Lantham: Alta Mir, 2011), 285–305.
53 Prabhu, personal communication, January 23, 2024.

Bibliography

Mamidipudi, Annapurna and Wiebe E. Bijker. "Innovation in Indian Handloom Weaving." *Technology and Culture* 59, no. 3 (July 2018): 509–545.

Norris, Lucy. "Creating Fame and Fortune from the Ruins of Handloom in Kerala, Southern India." In *Textile Economies: Power and Value from the Local to the Transitional*, 285–305. Lantham: Alta Mir, 2011.

Parthasarathi, Prasannan. *The Transition to a Colonial Economy: Weavers, Merchants and Kings in South India, 1720–1800*. No. 7. Cambridge: Cambridge University Press, 2001.

Ramanathan, Veerabhadran and Gregory Carmichael. "Global and Regional Climate Changes due to Black Carbon." *Nature Geoscience* 1, no. 4 (2008): 221–227.

8 Afterword

Parimal Bhattacharya writes in his book *Field Notes from a Waterborne Land*, how the Sundarbans stand for anything that is "sinking, threatened, delicate, fecund, fabled, uncanny, ancient and young – all these and more at the same time and in the same space".[1] In describing Sundarbans as a metaphor, Bhattacharya is also referring to places as a metaphor for fluidities of shifting faith, shifting identity and shifting land.[2]

The visual of the bare-chested body of the weaver, toiling away on the loom, glistening with sweat, remains etched in my mind. As the many discussions with the weavers in the three regions revealed, there were no direct answers as to how climate change is affecting their practice. The geographies witnessed varied types of changes and this was reflected in their responses too that were at times a derivative of the socio-political climate of the region or state. It was in understanding and questioning the micro-processes that more systemic issues came to the fore. In setting out to explore the vexing issue of climate change and attempting to locate its differential impacts across the three regions, I discovered alternative worlds that although slightly deranged from what I had initially set out to do but cannot be left divorced from the central issue. At the same time, while conducting fieldwork, it was difficult to decouple the effects of climate change on weaving societies from the general structural changes that the Indian handloom industry has been facing and the irrevocable decline it has been subjected to.

Mridula Ramesh in her book *The Climate Solution* writes, "Climate change is about so much more than just a simple increase of temperature. It is about shifting to a profoundly different world."[3] India is known to possess an abundant history of moderate lifestyle that relies on adapting to changing climate. In recording localised responses to climate change, the many possibilities in traditional knowledge were unveiled, thereby building upon the interrelationships between traditional knowledge and climate change. As city dwellers, we have a narrow understanding of the climate shift and are unable to look beyond vehicular emissions, power

DOI: 10.4324/9781003450061-8

fluctuations and water shortages. Kimmerer was right when she articulated this concern in *Braiding Sweetgrass* – "We set ourselves up as arbiters of what is good when often our standards of goodness are driven by narrow interests, by what we want."[4] Compared to a city dweller's nescience, the rural inhabitants, in their many ways of living, were replete with ancestral knowledge, of their indigeneity, complex native science and the 'durability of traditions'.[5]

The effects of climate change are omnipresent. One only needs to lend an ear to the many stories that the weavers and their communities hold. As Kimmerer says, "To learn again, you have to listen."[6] As it turned out in my discoveries, climate change was a cumulative effect of various factors – actions, habits and rituals were strung together to explain the phenomenon of climate change. The remoteness of the regions, particularly Kutch, was crucial in reinforcing how the changing climate impacts the vulnerable the most, particularly people on the margins in hot climates, as Ramesh discusses in *The Climate Solution*.[7]

Kutch is also a land formed by changing climatic conditions over the centuries. Between 1819 and 2001, the region was hit by ninety earthquakes in total, with the most recent one in 2001 that displaced over half a million.[8] The insularity of the region and the recurrent adaptions of the inhabitants to these shifts have made them holders of inveterate knowledge. My concerns resonate with the accelerating changes that might render regions such as Kutch as hotspots for 'clima-tourists', a term marine scientist Ellen Prager frames in her book *Dangerous Earth* to denote people who want to see climate change up, close and personal.[9]

It is predicted the warming will increase to such proportions that could force nearly 40 million people to migrate across the subcontinent as their homes would be rendered inhabitable.[10] The effects of migration would also lead to a restructuring of relationships as was seen in the study of women warpers in Kutch. Where these warpers in Kutch have formed such an important part of the weaving process, of late, as Judy Frater discusses, brides are brought from the cities, who do not know how to prepare warps or how to wind yarn on the bobbin for shuttles.[11]

Women as part of the weaving process have hitherto been discussed only in the context of spinning and rarely as weavers even though they constitute the largest number of weavers, particularly in regions such as the North East. Including a separate chapter on women and their contribution to the process of weaving was thus important. With more women taking up weaving within the paternalistic traditions, the book thus invites readers to rethink the idea of a craftsman or a weaver, amidst the gendered conversations on craft and the larger public imagination.

The social lives of South Asian weaver communities have remained fairly less explored, as Murari Jha also pointed out. The book thus forms a bridge by including research that has skipped the canons in Indian textile history. For instance, where textiles from other regions have received significant focus, textiles from Kerala have scarcely been recorded historically. Another problem with studies on handloom is that all credit goes to the weaver who is positioned much higher in the hierarchy of skills as compared to spinning or other ancillary tasks. This book was an attempt to dissect and unravel issues on the ground pertaining to weavers and their craft.

Notes

1 Piramal Bhattacharya, *Field Notes from a Waterborne Land: Bengal Beyond the Bhadralok* (India, Gurugram: Harper Collins, 2022), 28.
2 Bhattacharya, *Field Notes from a Waterborne Land*, 234.
3 Mridula Ramesh, *The Climate Solution: India's Climate-Change Crisis and What We Can Do About It* (India: Hachette India, 2019), 25.
4 Robin Wall Kimmerer, *Braiding Sweetgrass: Indigenous Wisdom, Scientific Knowledge and the Teachings of Plants* (UK: Penguin Books, 2020), 92.
5 Judy Frater, "Warp and Weft: Tradition and Change, Craftsmen and Innovation in Bhujodi," *Marg* 73, no. 4 (2022): 130–135.
6 Kimmerer, *Braiding Sweetgrass*, 53
7 Ramesh, *The Climate Solution*, 38.
8 Archana Shah, *Shifting Sands. Kutch: Textiles, Traditions, Transformations* (Bandhej Books, 2013), 35.
9 Ellen Prager, *Dangerous Earth: what we wish we knew about Volcanoes, Hurricanes, Climate Change, Earthquakes, and more* (India, Gurugram: HarperCollins, 2022), 28.
10 Ramesh, *The Climate Solution*, 5.
11 Judy Frater, "Warp and Weft".

Bibliography

Bhattacharya, Piramal. *Field Notes from a Waterborne Land: Bengal Beyond the Bhadralok*. India, Gurugram: Harper Collins, 2022.
Frater, Judy. "Warp and Weft: Tradition and Change, Craftsmen and Innovation in Bhujodi." *Marg* 73, no. 4 (2022): 130–135.
Kimmerer, Robin Wall. *Braiding Sweetgrass: Indigenous Wisdom, Scientific Knowledge and the Teachings of Plants*. UK: Penguin Books, 2020.

Prager, Ellen. *Dangerous Earth: What we Wish we Knew about Volcanoes, Hurricanes, Climate Change, Earthquakes, and more*. India, Gurugram: HarperCollins, 2022.

Ramesh, Mridula. *The Climate Solution: India's Climate-Change Crisis and What We Can Do about It*. India: Hachette India, 2019.

Shah, Archana. *Shifting Sands. Kutch: Textiles, Traditions, Transformations*. Bandhej Books, 2013.

Index

9781032584324

T - #0016 - 270525 - C0 - 216/138/7 [9] - CB - 9781032584324 - Gloss Lamination